# Book of Words

ISBN: 1 86476 363 9

AXIOM
AUSTRALIA

www.axiompublishing.com.au

Printed in Malaysia

# Book of Words

## Compiled by
## Michelle O'Regan

# CONTENTS

Language is the most massive
and inclusive art we know,
a mountainous and anonymous work
of unconscious generations.
Edward Sapir, 1921, *Language*, Ch 9

# FOREWORD

*Book of Words* is a *must read* for anyone who is curious and intrigued by the living language.

*Book of Words* is going to take you on a zany light-hearted exploration of English in celebration of its glorious fallibility.

*Flamboyant Words* sets the scene with panache and impetuosity — words singled out for their sheer *joie de vivre.*

*Befuddled?* — a demystification of common confusables — is a regular feature throughout the text e.g. breach/breech, biennial/biannual.

The ambiguities, *double entendres*, and sheer inanity of headlines, signage and instructions are paraded for your entertainment.

Latin and Franglais, roots, and other offerings from our linguistic origins are set before you as an exotic verbal smogasbord.

Every configuration of wordplay — palindromes, anagrams, aptonyms, pangrams — are featured.

If you are at a loss to know what these terms mean, turn at any time to *Linguistic Lingo* in the final pages, where explanations and examples are provided. Also, the Index includes the links to terms and sections.

*Book of Words* offers many examples of language curios, trivia and ephemera, definitions, idiomatic explanations and rule breakers.

Nonsense poems provide fine examples of the pitfalls of English spelling, plurals and pronunciation.

Did you know that an oxymoron, plural oxymora, is a 'contradiction in terms', *friendly fire* being one of the most notorious; that a pleonasm, such as *ATM machine,* is the opposite of an oxymoron?

How are these for animal collectives? A parliament of owls, a convocation of eagles, a rumpus of baboons?

Did you know that mnemonics is an aid for remembering things. *My Vicious Echidna Might Just Stab Us Now* is a way of remembering the planets, minus Pluto, the icy dwarf.

Immerse yourself in a plethora of phobias and 'ologies, eponyms, acronyms and pormanteaux (blend words), and where you will finish, nobody knows!

Fantastical words and freshly minted ones, buzzwords, jargon and euphemisms — they all pass across the proverbial stage for their moment of amusement and bemusement.

Language is akin to a coral reef teeming with life. The scuba diver descends beneath the ocean's surface to admire its beauty and diversity. We too can pause to appreciate and savour the linguistic richness, legacy of many a generation and culture, and wonder at its organic and convoluted complexities — at once wonderful, miraculous, ungovernable and imperfect as we ourselves are.

Words ...

reflections in the pools of our mind
cascading, sprawling,
teasing,
fluttering, echoing,
droning, splattering, stinging,
luxuriant,
opalescent, prim, obsequious,
iridescent,
turgid,
furious, exuberant,
flat, rigid, soft,
velvety.

— *Michelle O'Regan*

# FLAMBOYANT WORDS A - F

*What have these words in common? Their exuberance, irreverence and irrepressibility.*

*They have not just been invented, although you might wish that you had the gift to come up with such gems. In fact, some have been around for quite a while.*

**AKIMBO**
Arms bent at the elbow, hands on hips — body language of defiance and stubbornness.

**ARCIPLUVIAN**
Literally many-coloured, like a rainbow.

**BALLYHOO**
Exaggerated publicity or advertising.

**BALDERDASH**
Senseless talk, twaddle.

**BAMBOOZLE**
Trick or deceive or mislead someone.

**BIBLIOBIBULI**
People who read too much.

**BLATHERSKITE**
A noisy talker of blatant rubbish; foolish talk or nonsense.

**BODACIOUS**
Blatant, remarkable, audacious, impressive, or attractive.

**BOMBILATE**
To make a humming, buzzing sound.

**BOONDOGGLE**
An unnecessary or wasteful project.

**BOUSTROPHEDON**
Back and forth pattern.

**BROUHAHA**
A noisy argument or commotion.

## BUCKAROO
Is a special kind of cowboy distinguished by his manner and dress—probably comes from the Spanish *vaquero*

## BUGABOO
Something that causes baseless fear or worry; also, a false belief used to intimidate.

## CACHINNATORY
Relating to loud or immoderate laughter.

## CALLIPYGIAN
Having well-shaped buttocks.

## CANOODLE
To hug and kiss.

## CAPRICIOUS
Whimsical, fickle.

## CATAGLOTTISM
Kissing with the tongue. Oooh la la!

## COCKALORUM
A self-important, little man.

## COCKAMAMIE
Absurd, crazy.

## CODOLOGY
Nonsense.

## CODSWALLOP
More nonsense!

## CRAPULENCE
Discomfort from eating or drinking.

## CRUCIVERBALIST
A compiler or solver of crossword puzzles.

## DANDIPRAT
A silly, little fellow or urchin.

## DEUCED
Exceedingly, devilishly.

## DIDAPPER
One who disappears only to bob up again.

## DISCOMBOBULATED
Thrown into a state of confusion.

## DISEMBOGUEMENT
A discharging at the mouth, in a very rapid non-stop continuous action — in other words, running at the mouth.

## DOOZY
Refers to something extraordinary or outstanding of its kind. Thought to derive from the famous Eleanor Duse, an Italian actress at the end of the 1800s.

## DUMBLEDORE
A type of bee, and now the name of the Professor from the Harry Potter books.

## DROOGISH
Relating to the nature or attitudes of a member of a street gang.

## FAFF
To dither or fumble about.

## FIASCO
A disaster of high emotion—thought to derive from the word for the chianti bottle that has a wicker wrapping because it can't stand up on its own.

## FLABBERGASTED
Astonished, agape.

## FLAMBOYANT
Rich in colour, flashy.

## FLIBBERTIGIBBET
A frivolous, flighty, or excessively talkative person.

## FLUBDUB
Bombastic language.

## FLUMMOXED
Confused or perplexed.

# LOVELY, LILTING LINES

*Poets do it, playwrights do it! Occasionally ordinary mortals in the heat of love do it! Let's do it, let's Alliterate!*

*That's using words beginning with the same letter.*


Although I'd lie lapped up in linen
A deal I'd sweat and little earn
If I should live as live the neighbours,'
Cried the beggar, Billy Byrne;
Stretch bones till the daylight come
On great-grandfather's battered tomb.


From *Under the Round Tower,* William Butler Yeats

\*   \*   \*   \*   \*   \*

'Tis not the beam of her bright blue eye,
Nor the smile of her lip of rosy dye,
Nor the dark brown wreaths of her glossy hair,
Nor her changing cheek, so rich and rare.
Oh! these are the sweets of a fairy dream,
The changing hues of an April sky.
They fade like dew in the morning beam,
Or the passing zephyr's odour'd sigh.


Joseph Rodman Drake
*'Tis Not the Beam of Her Bright Blue Eye*


\*   \*   \*   \*   \*   \*

Touch each object you want to touch as if tomorrow your tactile sense would fail.


Helen Keller, *The Seeing See Little*

Bird of the bitter bright grey golden morn
Scarce risen upon the dusk of dolorous years,
First of us all and sweetest singer born
Whose far shrill note the world of new men hears
Cleave the cold shuddering shade as twilight clears;
When song new-born put off the old world's attire
And felt its tune on her changed lips expire,
Writ foremost on the roll of them that came
Fresh girt for service of the latter lyre,
Villon, our sad bad glad mad brother's name!

Algernon Charles Swinburne, *Ballad*
\*   \*   \*

The deep churned.
Something had happened down in the dim,
foggy-green depths.

Paul Annixter, *Battle in the Depths*
\*   \*   \*

Dawn is dim on the dark soft water,
Soft and passionate, dark and sweet.
Love's own self was the deep sea's daughter,
Fair and flawless from face to feet,
Hailed of all when the world was golden,
Loved of lovers whose names beholden
Thrill men's eyes as with light of olden
Days more glad than their flight was fleet.

Algernon Charles Swinburne
*The Swimmer's Dream*

# INITIAL BRIEFING

*Our modern world is littered with abbreviated terms.*
*An acronym qualifies by being a pronounceable abbreviation*
*often sourced from the initial letters of a phrase or sentence.*
*Warning — the following list was not chosen for its gravity!*

**ABATE**: A Brotherhood Against Totalitarian Enactments.

**ACA**: Action for Corporate Accountability.

**ADD**: Attention Deficit Disorder. A cousin of ADHD, Attention Deficit Hyperactive Disorder. No such thing as naughtiness or mischief any more in children. There must be a physiological or internal chemical explanation!

**AIDS**: Acquired Immune Deficiency Disorder.

**AIM**: Accuracy In Media.

**AFLO**: Another Flipping Learning Opportunity.

**ANA:** Animals Not Allowed. Refers as much to the furry kind as much as to the badly behaved human!

**AOS**: All Options Stink; a situation in which there is no optimum or ideal course of action.

**APIS**: Any Port In a Storm.

**ASTRO**: Always Stating The Really Obvious.

**BANANA**: Build Absolutely Nothing Anywhere Near Anyone. A person who is opposed to new real estate development, particularly projects close to their neighbourhood.

**BHAG**: Big, Hairy, Audacious Goal.

**BOB**: Best Of Best.

**BOOSTER**: Balanced, Observed, Objective, Specific, Timely, Enhancing, Relevant. A coaching acronym, of course!

**BRICs**: The countries of Brazil, Russia, India, and China viewed as a group of emerging economies with large potential markets.

**CAFE**: Corporate Average Fuel Economy.

**CAM**: Complementary and Alternative Medicine.

**CAVEs**: Citizens Against Virtually Everything.

**CHAOS**: Can't Have Anyone Over Syndrome; not inviting guests to one's house because it is too messy or cluttered.

**CHIC**: Cross-dresser Heterosexual Intersocial Club.

**CHOP**: Chauvinist, Hairy, Officious Pig.

**CIO:** Career Is Over.

**CLAWS:** Creating Liveable Alternatives to Wage Slavery.

**DAGMAR**: Defining Advertising Goals for Measured Advertising Realities - in other words, check the marketplace!

**DRIB**: Don't Read If Busy. Only the e-generation could have considered this necessary.

**DUPPIE:** A Depressed Urban Professional.

**ESO:** Equipment Superior to Operator. Shorthand for "There's nothing wrong with this equipment, the problem is with the owner."

**FAS:** Foetal Alcohol Syndrome.

**FIGJAM**: Flip I'm good, Just Ask Me!

**FILO**: First In, Last Out. A common approach to laying staff off.

**FINE**: F**ked, Insecure, Neurotic and Emotional.

**FLUF**: Fat, Little, Ugly Fellow.

**FOBIO**: Frequently Outwitted By Inanimate Objects.

**GALA**: Gay and Lesbian Alliance.

**GAAFOFY**: Go Away And Find Out For Yourself.

**GLAM**: Greying, Leisurely, Affluent Married.

**GOFERs**: Genial Old Farts Enjoying Retirement.

**GOOMBY:** Get Out Of My Back Yard! – someone who

seeks to remove or else stop some unpleasant feature from becoming a fixture in their neighbourhood.

**HIV**: Human Immunodeficiency Virus.

**IKIWISI**: I'll Know It When I See It.

**IMHO**: In My Humble Opinion.

**IMMLY**: Is My Medicine Legal Yet?

**JOOTT**: Just One Of Those Things. An unexplained computer problem that resolves itself over time or just by rebooting the machine.

**KIPPERS**: Kids in Parent's Pockets Eroding Retirement Savings.

**LIFE**: Lobby for Individual Freedom and Equality.

**LULU**: Locally Unwanted Land Use. A real estate development or other construction project to which the local residents are opposed.

**MADD**: Mothers Against Drunk Drivers.

**MOUT**: Military Operations in Urban Terrain.

**NEV**: A Neighbourhood Electric Vehicle; a small electric car designed to travel at low speeds over short distances.

**NOISE**: The adversaries and enemies of Microsoft: Netscape, Oracle, IBM, Sun, and Everyone else.

**NORC**: Naturally Occurring Retirement Community; an apartment building or neighborhood where most of the residents have grown old.

**NOTE**: Not Over There, Either. A person or attitude that opposes new real estate development in the local community and is not open to compromise on this issue.

**NUMBY**: Not Under My Back Yard; a person who hopes or seeks to keep some dangerous or unpleasant underground feature out of his or her neighborhood; the attitude of such a person.

**RAM**: Random Access Memory. Not to be confused with ROM Read Only Memory.

**OTPOTSS:** Orientation Towards People Of The Same Sex. This is intended as a replacement for the word *homosexual* in the Department of Trade and Industry in England as it was felt that homosexual was 'no longer the way forward in defining sexual orientation'

**RIF**: Reduction in force. The company underwent an RIF.

**SAD**: Seasonal Affective Disorder. The kind of depression that hits sufferers in the winter months.

**SAR**: Specific Absorption Rate: the rate at which the electromagnetic radiation emissions from a cell phone or other wireless device are absorbed by bodily tissue.

**SARS**: Severe Acute Respiratory Syndrome; a highly contagious, pneumonia-like illness with symptoms that include high fever, shortness of breath, and coughing.

**SIDS:** Sudden Infant Death Syndrome.

**SIEV**: Suspected Illegal Entry Vessel. The Australian Government's acronym for boat people's vessels.

**SITCOM**: Single Income, Two Children, Oppressive Mortgage. The natural evolution of upwardly-mobile couples who have children and then one spouse stops working to raise the kids.

**SNAG:** Sensitive New Age Guy.

**SODDI Defense**: Some Other Dude Did It. In law, the defense team that makes an argument that there were any other numbers of individuals who could have done the crime their client is being charged with.

**TEOTWAWKI**: The End Of The World As We Know It; a catch-all phrase for the chaos and disruption that some people expect will occur in the new millennium.

**URL**: Unable to Readily Locate.

**YUPPIE**: Young Urban Professional.

# READ ALL ABOUT IT!

*What hope is there for mere mortal word- amateurs, when the professional wordsmiths make such clangingly obvious double entendres an inadvertent typos.*

*These are headlines taken from real newspapers:*

Prostitutes appeal to Pope.

Stiff opposition expected to casketless funeral plan.

Men recommend more clubs for wives.

Two convicts evade noose; jury hung.

Traffic dead rise slowly.

Dr. Ruth to talk about sex with newspaper editors.

Sterilisation solves problems for pets, owners.

British left waffles on Falkland islands.

Lung cancer in women mushrooms.

City pacts fight boils.

Eye drops off shelf.

Teacher strikes idle kids.

Squad helps dog bite victim.

Module's offensive looks hard to beat.

American ships head to Libya.

Lawyers give poor free legal advice.

Doctors help torch victim.

Milk drinkers are turning to powder.

Town to drop school bus when overpass is ready.

Genetic engineering splits scientists.

Queen Mary having bottom scraped.

Connie tied, nude policeman testifies.

Calf born to farmer with two heads.

Police can't stop gambling.

Headless body found in topless bar.

Severed head offers few answers.

Man is charged with killing his missing wife.

Grandmother of eight makes hole in one.

New study of obesity looks for larger test group.

Carolina inn loses license for racism.

Steals clock, faces time.

Cervical cancer linked to smoking in a study.

Reagan to have tissue removed from nose.

Dentist receives plaque.

Gorillas vow to kill Khomeini.

Some women lose breasts, find self-esteem.

Rain clouds welcome at airport.

Police act to stop urinating in public.

Press tours ravaged city.

Progress slow in beating death.

Man found beaten, robbed by police.

Cemetery allows people to be buried by their pets.

Boy hurt in accident in intensive care.

X-rays of Dean's head reveal nothing.

Eligible pet owners can get free neutering.

Woman born February 29 has baby same day.

Men burst in home, steal cash.

Eight American men left.

For ninth time in 2 years, Leominster teen dies violently.

Two-headed baby recalls similar birth in 1970.

Fireproof clothing factory burns to ground.

Infant morality shows drop here.

Sues bride of four mouths.

Hotel burns. 200 guests escape half glad.

Many Maine women live under the treat of domestic violence.

Socks lower in Tokyo.

Crowds rushing to see Pope trample 6 to death.

Sudden rush to help people out of work.

Serious crime down, but murders increase.

Another body found missing.

Woman commits suicide, sets car afire.

Two teenagers indicted for drowning in lake.

Death of Bette Davis brings flood of praise.

A grateful nation buries Sam Rayburn.

Columbus discovered virgins and they are still fascinating.

Former state trooper loses appeal in sex case.

Woman to drop suit for sperm.

Women sought for state police.

Beauty queen unveils bust at dedication ceremony.

Father of 9 fined $100 for failing to stop.

Do-it-yourself pregnancy kit to go on sale.

Judge to rule on nude beach.

# THINGAMAJIG

*On how many occasions do we struggle for the names of little things? Either we learnt it, and quickly forgot, or we never knew because we didn't need to know and weren't interested to find out. Here are just a few:*

BELT: tongue, punch holes, keeper
BROOM: neck (where handle attached to broom)
CLOTHES PEG: grinning hole, claw end
COMB: spine, teeth
DOOR: lintel, jamb, threshold
EYEGLASSES: eye wires (surround glass), budge (bridges the nose), temples (hook over ears)
HAIR DRYER: barrel, air vents
HAT: brim, crown
NAIL: shank, head
PADLOCK: shackle (movable arched bar)
PAIL: ears (where handle attaches to pail)
PAPER CLIPS: legs (straight), bends (rounded)
SAFETY PIN: shaft
SCISSORS: blades, pivot, bow handle (large), ring handle (small)
SHOE: aglet (tip of shoelace), welt (between upper and sole), counter (back panel)
SOCK: toe, gore (back)
STAIRS: tread, riser, railing, banister, newel post
STAPLE: crown, legs
TOOTHBRUSH: block handle, block head (where bristles are inserted)
WINDOW: lintel, sill, panes, sash
ZIPPER: pull tab, slide, teeth

*Synonyms for thingamajig — doohickey, gizmo, thingamabob, doodad, widget, whatsis, thingumabob, whatchamacallit, oojah*
*... can you think of other thingamies for whatsits?*

# STRANGE INSTRUCTIONS

*Life can be stranger than fiction!*

*Especially when it comes to written instructions. After all, we live in litigious times. One assumes a modicum of common sense at one's peril.*

Caution: remove infant before folding — *On a child's stroller*

Keep away from children — *On a bottle of baby lotion*

Warning: sharp blades — *On a packet of craft knives*

Do not peel label off— *On the back of a drink bottle label*

Do not aim at your face — *On a can of spray paint*

Aim towards the enemy — *Printed on a US Army rocket launcher*

Remove plastic before eating — *On a snack bar wrapper*

Do not insert curling iron into any bodily orifice — *On a curling iron*

Caution: hot beverages are hot — *On a takeaway coffee cup*

For best results, start with clean bathtub before use — *On a bath cleaning agent*

Warning: misuse may cause injury or death
        — *On the barrel of a .22-calibre rifle*

Caution — do not swallow nails. Will cause irritation
— *On a box of nails*

For serious injuries, seek medical attention
— *On a packet of band aids*

Warning: do not insert fingers — *On a blender*

Warning: high in sodium — *On a packet of salt*

Mix with water before serving
— *On a can of infant formula powder*

Remove wrapper, open mouth, insert muffin, eat
— *On a muffin packet*

Instructions: put on food — *On a ketchup bottle*

Open bottle before drinking — *On a bottle of rum*

This product not intended for use as dental drill — *On an electrical rotary device*

Warning: Flammable — *On a container of lighter fluid*

Do not eat toner — *On a toner cartridge*

On the bottom of a Coca Cola bottle — *Do not open here*

Beware of people — *Sign in a street in Hong Kong*

Safe for use around pets — *On a packet of kitty litter*

Do not blow dry in sleep — *On a hair dryer*

First, carry to fire — *On a fire extinguisher*

Caution: the contents of this bottle should not be fed to fish
— *On a bottle of dog shampoo*

Warning: When motor is running, blade is turning
— *On a lawnmower*

Do not use intimately — *On a can of deodorant*

Do not use as an ice cream topping — *On a bottle of hair dye*

Do not use under water — *On a toaster*

Do not allow children to play in the dishwasher
— *On a dishwasher*

Caution: do not use this hammer to strike any solid object
— *On the handle of a hammer*

Protect from seawater — *On an ocean buoy*

Caution: May cause drowsiness, do not drive or operate heavy
machinery — *On a bottle of children's cough medicine*

Do not spray into electrical outlet — *On a hose nozzle*

May irritate eyes — *On a can of pepper spray*

Caution: contents hot — *On a Domino's Pizza box*

Do not use orally. — *On a toilet brush*

Please keep out of children. — *On a butcher's knife*

Not suitable for children 36 months or less.
    *— On a 1 year old's birthday card*

Keep out of reach of children and teenagers.
    *— On a can of air freshener*

For use on animals only. — *On an electric cattle prod*

Do not use for drying pets.
    *—- In the manual for a microwave oven*

Remember, objects in the mirror are actually behind you.
  *—- On a motorcycle helmet-mounted rear-view mirror*

Do not use as ear plugs. —- *On a package of silly putty*

Not for weight control. —- *On a pack of Breath Savers*

Has been known to cause cancer in laboratory rats.
    *— On a container of rat poison*

Do not iron clothes on body. —- *On packaging for an iron*

Product will be hot after heating.
    *— On a Marks & Spencer bread pudding*

# A NAG'S ARM

*If you can take a name or a word and jumble the letters to form another word or phrase, then you've made an anagram. A nag's arm is an anagram for anagrams!*

| | |
|---|---|
| A Gentleman | Elegant Man |
| A Domesticated Animal | Docile, As A Man Tamed It |
| Alien Abductions | Tabloid Nuisance |
| Animosity | Is No Amity |
| Banana Republic | Annual Bribe Cap |
| Barbie Doll | Liberal Bod |
| Boeing | Big One |
| Butterfly | Flutter-by |
| Cigarette Advertising | Creating Grave Ditties |
| Circumstantial Evidence | Can Ruin A Selected Victim |
| Contradiction | Accord Not In It |
| Conversation | Voices Rant On |
| Debit Card | Bad Credit |
| Election Results | Let's Recount |
| Exclamation | A Climax |
| Florence Nightingale | Nigel, Fetch An Iron Leg |
| Greyhound | Hey, Dog, Run! |
| Intoxicate | Excitation |
| Lifesavers | Safer Lives |
| Mediocrity | Me Cry "Idiot" |
| Natural Voices | Saliva Counter |
| Parliament | Partial Men |
| Pre-natal | Parental |
| Presbyterian | Best In Prayer |
| Prognosis | Signs: Poor |
| Random House | Around Homes |
| Real Networks | Lowest Ranker |
| Schoolmaster | The Classroom |
| Silence of the Lambs | Con Bites Male Flesh |
| Software | Swear Oft |

| | |
|---|---|
| Sustainable energy | Sane, suitably green. |
| The Detectives | Detect Thieves |
| The Earthquakes | That Queer Shake |
| The Enron Corporation | Horror! Note Panic Tone! |
| The Eyes | They See |
| The Google Search Engine | Oh, Cheer Net-Logging Ease! |
| The Hilton | Hint: Hotel |
| The Hospital Ambulance | A Cab, I Hustle to Help Man |
| The Intel Corporation | Tailor One Rotten Chip |

## SOME BIG NAMES

| | |
|---|---|
| Donald Rumsfeld | Dullards if demon |
| President Bush | Burnished pest |
| Anthony Blair | Tory Hannibal |
| John Winston Howard | Join harsh down-town |
| Tony Blair PM | I'm Tory plan B |
| Hillary Clinton | Only I can thrill |

## FOOD STUFFS

| | |
|---|---|
| Bangers and mash | Bad man gnashers |
| Eggs and bacon | Conned gasbag |
| Sweet and sour pork | Outspoken rewards |
| Rhubarb crumble | Rubber club harm |
| Cornish charter pie | Protein rich search |
| Stuffed sardines | Disaster snuffed |
| Fried noodles | Defines drool |

# BEFUDDLED?

*All ready / Already*
All ready means "all prepared"
Already means "before a stated or expected time"

*Alternate / Alternative*
Alternate means "every other one"
Alternative means "another choice or possibility"

# DOES THIS COMPUTE?

The dot over the letter "I" is called a *tittle*.

The # key on the keyboard is called an *octothorpe*.

The squiggly line ~ has a name: *tilde*.

The name for the "&" meaning "and" is *ampersand*.

The slash character / is called a *virgule, or solidus.*

The < > are called angle braces.

Using        for text left out or fading ending is called an ellipsis.

` is called a grave or grave accent.

These symbols { } are called braces.

Whereas these [ ] are brackets.

^ is a circumflex or a caret.

# ENOUGH, ENOUGH!

The wind was rough
And cold and blough;
She kept her hands inside her mough.
It chilled her through,
Her nose turned blough,
And still the squall the faster flough.

And yet although
There was no snough,
The weather was a cruel fough.
It made her cough,
(Please do not scough);
She coughed until her hat blew ough.

- *author unknown*

# LATIN SAYINGS

Fiat justitia; ruat coelum;
*Let justice be done;*
*though heaven fall.*

Tempus fugit et nos fugimus in illus.
*Time flies and we fly with it.*

Ars Longa, Vita Brevis
*A real work of art will outlive its creator.*
— Hippocrates

Difficile est satiram non scribere.
*It is difficult not to write satire.*
— Juvenal

Nullius in verba
*Take no-one's word for it.*

Quid me nutrit me destruit
*What nourishes me also destroys me.*

Si vis pacem, para bellum
*If you want peace, prepare for war.*

Illiud Latine dici non potest
*You can't say that in Latin.*

Cogito, ergo sum
*I think, therefore I am.*

# ANIMALS: FLOCKS 'N' CHICKS

| Animal | Collective Noun | Offspring |
|---|---|---|
| alligator | congregation | hatchling |
| antelope | herd | calf |
| ant | army, colony, swarm | antling |
| ape | shrewness | infant |
| baboon | rumpus | infant |
| badger | cete | kit, cub |
| bat | cloud | bitten, pup |
| bear | sleuth, sloth | cub |
| beaver | colony, lodge | kit, kitten |
| bee | hive, grist, swarm | larva |
| bird | congregation, flock, dissimulation, volary | chick, hatchling |
| bittern | sedge, sledge | chick |
| buffalo | herd | calf |
| butterfly | flutter | caterpillar |
| buzzard | wake | chick |
| camel | flock | calf |
| cat | clowder, clutter | kit, kitten |
| cattle | drove, herd | calves |
| chimpanzee | cartload | infant |
| cockroach | intrusion | larva |
| codfish | | codling |
| coot | cover | hatchling |
| cow | herd | calf (calves) |
| coyote | band, pack, shift, wiliness | pup |
| crane | herd, sedge, sledge | hatchling, chick, colt |
| deer | herd | fawn, yearling |
| dog | pack | pup, whelp |
| dolphin | pod | calf |
| donkey | drove, herd | foal |
| dove | dule | squab |
| duck | flock (in air), paddling (on water), team | duckling |

| Animal | Collective Noun | Offspring |
|---|---|---|
| eagle | convocation | eaglet, eyas |
| echidna | | puggle |
| eel | swarm | elver |
| elephant | herd, parade | calf |
| elephant seal | pod | yearling/weaner |
| elk | gang | calf |
| emu | mob | chick, hatchling |
| ferret | business, fesnyng | kit |
| fish | catch, drought, haul, run, school, shoal | fry, fingerling |
| fly | business, swarm | maggot |
| fox | leash, skulk | cub, kit, pup |
| frog | army | polliwog, tadpole |
| giraffe | corps, herd, totter, tower | calf |
| goat | flock, tribe, trip | kid |
| goose | gaggle/skein | cheeper, gosling grouse |
| gorilla | band | infant |
| grouse | drumming | cheeper, chick |
| hare | down, husk | |
| hawk | cast, kettle | fledgling, eyas |
| hedgehog | array | piglet |
| hen | brood | chick |
| hippo | bloat | calf |
| hornet | nest | larva |
| horse | herd, ramuda, string | foal, (colt *m*, filly *f*), yearling |
| hound | cry, mute, pack | pup |
| hummingbird | charm | chick |
| hyena | cackle | |
| insect | swarm | larva, nymph |
| jackrabbit | husk | |
| kangaroo | mob, troop | joey |
| lapwing | deceit | |
| lark | ascension, exaltation | chick |

| Animal | Collective Noun | Offspring |
| --- | --- | --- |
| leopard | leap, leep | cub |
| lion | pride | cub |
| locust | plague | larva |
| louse | colony | nit |
| mallard | sord | duckling |
| marten | richness | chick |
| mole | labor | pup |
| monkey | troup | infant |
| moose | herd | calf |
| mosquito | swarm | nymph |
| mouse | hoard, mischief | pinky |
| mule | barren, span | foal |
| nightingale | watch | chick |
| owl | parliament | owlet |
| ox | drove, herd, team, yoke | calf |
| oyster | bed | spat |
| parrot | company, flock | chick |
| partridge | covey | cheeper, chick |
| peacock/ peafowl | muster, ostentation | peachick |
| penguin | rookery | chick |
| pheasant | bouquet, nide, nye | chick |
| pig | litter | farrow, piglet, shoat, suckling |
| pigeon | flight, flock | squab, squeaker |
| polar bear | pack | cub |
| porcupine | prickle | cub |
| porpoise | herd, pod | calf |
| prairie dog | coterie | pup |
| quail | bevy, covey | cheeper, chick |
| rabbit | nest, warren | bunny |
| raccoon | nursery | cub |
| rat | hoard, mischief, pack, swarm | pinky, pup |
| rhino | crash | calf |
| sea gull | colony | chick |
| seal | colony, herd, pod | pup |

| Animal | Collective Noun | Offspring |
|---|---|---|
| shark | school, shiver | cub, pup |
| sheep | flock | cosset, hog, lamb, lambkins |
| skunk | surfeit | kit |
| snake | bed, nest, pit, rave | snakelet, hatchling |
| sparrow | flight, host | chick |
| spider | clutter, cluster | spiderling |
| squirrel | scurry | pup |
| starling | murmuration | chick |
| stork | mustering | chick |
| swallow | flight | chick |
| swan | bevy, herd, lamentation, team, wedge | cygnet |
| thrush | mutation | chick |
| tiger | ambush, streak | cub, whelp |
| toad | knot | tadpole, polliwog |
| trout | hover | fry, fingerling |
| turkey | flock, gang, raft, rafter | poult |
| turtledove | dule, pitying | chick |
| turtle | bale. | hatchling |
| whale | gam, school, pod | calf |
| viper | generation, nest | snakelet |
| wolf | herd, pack, route | pup, whelp |

Whales have calves,
Cats have kittens,
Bears have cubs,
Bats have bittens
Swans have cynets,
Seals have puppies,
But guppies just have little guppies!

— *Ogden Nash*

# CHRIS CROSS,
# PUZZLE POSER

*When a person's name is a canny match for their occupation it's called an aptonym.*

*Here are examples of real matchers!*

| | |
|---|---|
| I M. Babey | Paediatrician |
| Candy Baggs | Confectionary sales |
| John Bagwell | Anaesthesiologist |
| Ava Ball | Wedding planner |
| Robin Banks | Credit card specialist |
| Diane Berry | Mortician |
| Yolanda Bigwan | Fishing guide |
| David Bird | Ornithologist |
| Jett Black | Hair stylist |
| Dr. Bjerk | Psychiatrist |
| Drs. Blood and Gore | Surgeons |
| Alan Bloom | Gardener |
| Rita Book | Medical librarian |
| Bill Bord | Sign painter |
| Dr. Borer | Emergency medicine |
| Dr. Bowser | Veterinarian |
| Dr. Russell Brain | Neurologist |
| Iain Cash | Cashier |
| Dr. Richard Chopp | Urologist |
| Dr. Donald Chui | Dentist |
| Scott Constable | Police officer |
| Noah Count | Voting statistician |
| Chris Cross | Puzzle guru |
| Bertha de Bleus | Jazz singer |
| Doctor D'Eath | Surgeon |

| | |
|---|---|
| Dr. Dement | Psychiatrist |
| Leonard Divine | Rabbi |
| Doolittle & Dalley | Real estate agents |
| Eileen Dover | Compliant bimbo |
| Creflo A. Dollar | T.V. Evangelist |
| Will Dunn | Lawyer |
| Mustapha Fagg | Tobacco addict |
| Alexander Garden | Botanist |
| Morris Glaser | Glass company founder |
| Polly Glott | Translator |
| Donald Goodness | Rector |
| Roy Grout | Tiler |
| Steven Haddock | Aquarium Research |
| Cliff Hanger | Serial writer |
| Harcourt Champion | Wimbledon pro |
| John Hedges | Bank trader |
| Dr. Henry Head | Neurologist |
| Mr. Horn | Band teacher |
| Nita House | Real estate agent |
| Claire Jewell | Gemmologist |
| Dr. Korn | Podiatrist |
| Dr. Kutteroff | General Practitioner |
| Noah Lott | Encyclopaedist |
| Philip McCavity | Dentist |
| Dr. Michelle Moller | Dentist |
| Jim Nast | Parallel bars champion |
| Marian Nett | Puppeteer |
| Otto Nogo | Mechanic |
| Les Noyes | Sound consultant |
| Dr. Nurse | General Practitioner |
| Dr. Nutt | Psychiatrist |
| Malcolm Plumb | Plumber |

| | |
|---|---|
| Dr. Popwell | Chiropractor |
| Francine Prose | Writer |
| Horst Rayner | Equestrian |
| Dr. Wong See | Optometrist |
| Sonia Shears | Hairdresser |
| Coral Shore | Swimmer |
| Hy Singer | Castrato |
| Dr. Slaughter | Surgeon |
| Raymond Strike | Union president |
| Wayne Spillman | Lubrication engineer |
| Dr. Stopp | Surgeon |
| Sudds Family | Washing/cutting dog hair |
| Swindells & Gentry | Chartered accountants |
| S. Tait | Probate lawyer |
| Tess Tament | Probate lawyer |
| Philip D. Tank | Service station attendant |
| Dr. Richard Tapper | Urologist |
| Jess Tation | Obstetrician |
| Imogene Tensifier | Infra-red optical instrument specialist |
| Marion Tester | Water sample analyst |
| Dr. Julie Theorem | Mathematics professor |
| Cass Toff | Second-hand clothes dealer |
| Oliver Towne | Social columnist |
| Dr. Tranquilli | Anaesthesiologist |
| Henrietta Wilde | Zoologist |

# BODY LANGUAGE

The groove running between your nose and lips is called the *philtrum.*

If someone is *gabbertushed* they have buck teeth.

*Sternutation* is the act of sneezing.

The little lump of flesh just forward of your ear canal, right next to your temple, is called a *tragus.*

If a person is *wallopy* then they are loose-limbed.

If you're *leptodactylous* you have long slender toes.

*Dipsomania* means an insatiable craving for alcohol.

If you're *diastemic*, you have a gap between your teeth.

Hairy people are *hirsute.*

*Palmiped* describes a web-footed condition.

*Cock-throppled* means a man has a very large Adam's apple.

If someone is *hyperosmic,* they have a keen sense of smell.

If you're a vision of *pulchritude*, you're beautiful.

Tummy rumbles have a name – *borborygmi*

If you've just *nictated* then you've winked.

*Snaggletoothed* describes the condition of a jutting tooth.

Someone with a projecting chin is *gash-gabbit.*

*Peristalsis* is the involuntary muscle-wave in the digestive tract.

*Pandiculation* is act of stretching and yawning

A toothless person is *edentate or agomphious.*

If a person has a double chin or bulbous cheeks, they are *bucculent.*

*Dactylic* means concerning the fingers.

A *dolichopodous* person has long feet.

# SIGN OF THE TIMES

*You see them here, you see them there, you see those weird signs everywhere - don't you worry, don't you fret, laugh a little but don't forget!*

**In the window of a dry cleaner's:**
Same day dry cleaning — all garments ready in 48 hours

**At the zoo:**
Please do not feed the elephants. If you have any peanuts or buns give them to the keeper on duty

**Traffic sign:**
Parking restricted to 60 minutes in any hour

**In an office:**
After teabreak staff should empty the teapot and stand upside down on the draining board

**Outside a furniture shop:**
Our motto: We promise you the lowest prices and workmanship

**In a grocery shop:**
Try our local butter. Nobody can touch it

**Outside a farm:**
Cattle please close gate

**Sign outside a new town hall which was to be opened by the Prince of Wales:**
The town hall is closed until opening. It will remain closed after being opened. Open tomorrow

**Outside a photographer's studio:**
Out to lunch: if not back by five, out for dinner also

**Sign on a farm gate:**
Dogs found worrying will be shot

**In a restaurant:**
Customers who find our waiting staff rude should see the manager

**Seen at the side of a Sussex road:**
Slow cattle crossing. No overtaking for the next 100 yrs.

**Seen outside a travel agency:**
Why don't you go away?

**Notice in a pet shop:**
Birds going cheep!

**Outside a disco:**
Smarts is the most exclusive disco in town. Everyone welcome

**In an electrical shop:**
Why smash your plates washing up? Let one of our dishwashers do it for you

**Sign at a garden fete:**
Baby show. All entries to be handed in at the gate

**In a cafe window:**
Waitresses required for breakfast

**Notice in a London park:**
No walking, sitting or playing on the grass in this pleasure park

**Seen in a Coventry Factory:**
Any member of staff who needs to take the day off to go to a funeral must warn the foreman on the morning of the match

**Spotted in a garden centre:**
Up these steps for the sunken garden

**Sign on a newly painted bench:**
Wet paint. Watch it or wear it

**Seen in a watch shop:**
Please wait patiently to be served. I only have two hands

**Notice in the window of a fabric shop:**
Repairs and alterations done here. Dying arranged

**Road sign:**
Steeple Bumstead: Left 3 miles Right 3 miles
Straight ahead 3 miles

**Sign outside pet shop:**
No dogs allowed

**Notice in a dry cleaner's window:**
Anyone leaving their garments here for more than 30 days will be disposed of

**Spotted in a Blackpool guest house:**
Hot and cold running in all rooms

**Notice in Keighley restaurant:**
From Monday our catering assistants will be pleased to serve customers to the vegetables

**Seen outside a fire station:**
Fire Station - No Smoking

**Notice on Norfolk village shop:**
Half-day closing all day Wednesday

**Sign in London pizza parlour:**
Open 24 hours - except 2 a.m. – 8 a.m.

**Seen outside dancing academy:**
Please mind the steps

**Sign on motorway garage:**
Please do not smoke near our petrol pumps. Your life may not be worth much but our petrol is

**Notice in health food shop window:**
Closed due to illness

**Spotted in a safari park:**
Elephants please stay in your car

**Circus poster:**
Biffo Brothers' Circus, featuring Marvo, the Strongest Man in the World. In town all weak

**Seen during a conference:**
For anyone who has children and doesn't know it, there is a day care on the first floor

**Sign in a tea shop:**
Today's special. Pot of tea with stones and jam

**Spotted in a golf club:**
Golfers please do not drink and drive

**Seen in a college:**
This week's lecture: Underwater Life by Peter Fish

**Notice in hairdresser's window:**
Stylist wanted. Good pay and fringe benefits

**Notice in a field:**
The farmer allows walkers to cross the field for free, but the bull charges

**Sign at the tennis club:**
Would spectators please be quiet during matches and let the players raise a racquet

**Spotted at the railway station:**
Passengers are asked not to cross the lines - it takes ages for us to uncross them again

**Notice at the zoo:**
Children found straying will be sent to the lion enclosure

**Message on a leaflet:**
If you cannot read, this leaflet will tell you how to get lessons

**Sign on a repair shop door:**
We can repair anything. (Please knock hard on the door — the bell doesn't work)

**Notice in church hall:**
Electrical specialist will be here on Thursday morning to show parishioners how to wire plugs and make small repairs. Followed by a light lunch

**Spotted in a toilet in a London office block:**
Toilet out of order. Please use floor below

**Sign in a Japanese hotel:**
Sports jackets may be worn but no trousers

**Sign in Swiss hotel:**
Do you wish to change in Zurich? Do so at the hotel bank!

**Sign in Italian hotel:**
Do not adjust your light hanger. If you wish more light see manager.

**Sign in Portuguese hotel:**
In case of fire please do your utmost to alarm the hall porter

**On a road sign:**
Caution: water on road during rain

# "A DRINK TO YOUR HEALTH!"

*This book is a jaunt through the English language, however let's digress and find out how other cultures toast each other.*

| | |
|---|---|
| Afrikaans | Gesondheid |
| Albanian | Shëndeti tuaj |
| Arabic | Fi sahitak |
| Armenian | Genatset |
| Austrian | Zum Wohl |
| Basque | Topa |
| Bengali | Joy |
| Bosnian | Zivjeli |
| Bulgarian | Nazdrave |
| Chinese | Kong chien |
| Cornish | Yeghes da |
| Croatian | Zivjeli / U zdravlje |
| Czech | Na zdraví |
| Danish | Skål |
| Dutch | Proost |
| Egyptian | Fee sihetak |
| Esperanto | Sanon |
| Estonian | Teie terviseks |
| Farsi | Ba'sal'a'ma'ti |
| Finnish | Kippis |
| Flemish | Op uw gezonheid |
| French | À votre santé / Santé |
| German | Prost |
| Greek | Gia'sou |
| Greenlandic | Kasugta |
| Hebrew | Le'chaim |
| Hindi | Apki Lambi Umar Ke Liye |
| Holooe | Kam-poe |
| Ido | Ye vua saneso |
| Irish Gaelic | Sláinte 1 |
| Italian | Salute / Cin cin |
| Japanese | Kampai |
| Korean | Konbe |

| | |
|---|---|
| Hungarian | Egészségedre |
| Icelandic | Santanka nu / Skål |
| Irish Gaelic | Sláinte |
| Italian | Salute /Cin cin |
| Japanese | Kampai |
| Korean | Konbe |
| Latvian | Prieka |
| Lithuanian | I sveikata |
| Malaysian | Minum |
| Mandarin | Gan bei |
| Mexican | Salud |
| Moroccan | Saha wa'afiab |
| Norwegian | Skål |
| Occitan | A la vòstra |
| Pakistani | Sanda bashi |
| Polish | Na zdrowie |
| Portuguese | Saúde |
| Rumanian | Noroc |
| Russian | Vashe zdorovie |
| Serbian | Zivjeli / U zdravlje |
| Sesotho | Nqa |
| Slovak | Na zdravie |
| Slovenian | Na zdravje |
| Spanish | Salud |
| Swahili | Afya / Vifijo |
| Swedish | Skål |
| Tagalog | Mabuhay |
| Thai | Chook-die / Sawasdi |
| Turkish | Serefe |
| Ukrainian | Na zdorov'ya |
| Welsh | Iechyd da |
| Yugoslavian | Ziveo / Ziveli |
| Zulu | Oogy wawa |

# MILLENNIUM BUZZWORDS

Words are a mirror of their times.
By looking at the areas in which the vocabulary
of a language is expanding fastest in a given period,
we can form a fairly accurate
impression of the chief preoccupations of society
at that time and the points at which
the boundaries of human endeavour
are being advanced.
— *John Ayto*

*Here are some catch phrases for our contemporary realities — consummate consumerism, the Net, advertising ebola and the brave new work place.*

**Alpha pups:** Kids, mini trend-setters, who spread *meme viruses.* (Memes are units of cultural information transmitted from one mind to another)

**Attention spam:** How long it takes to realise this email is just junk.

**Aural branding:** The notion that a sound can belong to a company.

**Brand conscious babies:** The new consumer pundit wisdom is that children can learn brand loyalty from as early as six months old — babies have been known to utter that brand name before Mama or Papa!

**Brandalism:** The way that libraries, art galleries etc. now have their walls defaced with the logos of their corporate sponsors.

**Brain dump:** Another way of saying 'brainstorming' only it does seem to carry some excretal connotations.

**Captive Kidspace:** The kind of places from which kids cannot run or hide, where advertisers can influence the patterns of future consumption e.g. selling Coke and crisps in schools.

**Career-limiting move (CLM):** A euphemism for foot-in-mouth or for being in the wrong place at the wrong time e.g. slagging your boss when he's just walked up behind you.

**Circling the drain:** What happens before you leave an organisation, marking time waiting for the best redundancy offer, maybe.

**Conspicuous non-consumption:** The kind of snobbery indicated by the list of things one would never buy "Oh we'd never get a big-screen TV"

**Core competencies:** This is supposed to be the non-negotiable stuff that you or the company are good at. It's a pet phrase that gets flogged to death without meaning much of anything.

**Corporate icon:** Like the Nike tick, this is supposed to be a symbol of everything the company stands for, its very soul.

**Corporate vanity publishing:** The kinds of glossy publications that businesses are willing to pay vast sums for to showcase their vision, mission and other delights. In effect, the only readers will be the proofreaders!

**Cradle-to-grave marketing:** Those child psychologists are working hard with huge budgets to ensure that babies will be brand loyal all through their lives.

**Culturally appropriate:** This is the excuse that First worlders use when there are inequities with the Third world e.g. a discrepancy in the wages paid to Mexican auto workers as opposed to their US counterparts. Reason? Because the salaries are culturally appropriate.

**Cyclosis:** The affliction that hits CEOs when they discover in a moment of blinding clarity that the company's boom in the last decade had everything to do with a favourable economic cycle and that a trained baboon could have steered the ship safely!

**Deceptionist:** The receptionist whose role is to run "static" for her boss or bosses to ensure that it's as hard as possible to gain access to them. Lie, cheat, intimidate — she will use every trick in the book!

**Deja-moo:** Bullshit again! And you get the feeling you've heard it all before.

**Designosaurs:** Designers who are luddites and refuse to use computer technology, could soon become extinct just like the 'giant lizards'

**Dumbing up:** Looking at junk culture, for instance reality TV, with the kind of intellectual probity one would normally have reserved for Shakespeare.

**Egosurfing:** "Googling" your own name and visiting the sites to see how widespread your fame is on the Net.

**Educrat:** Someone who works in the field of education without ever teaching a day in their lives. Those who can do, those who can't teach, and those who can't teach, work in education!

**Extreme tourism:** The one-upmanship of wanting to go where no one has been before or dare to travel to the last place anyone on Earth would go e.g. Iraq in wartime.

**Fart blanche:** The mistaken (usually male) belief that it's possible to fart in any place, no matter how hallowed, without being detected.

**Flashpacker:** Those spoilt rich kids who backpack, armed with their Amex cards and believe that the very act of travel makes them interesting.

**Foyerfication:** The act of tarting up entrances and foyers, using big name architects, on rather sad 60s and 70s office buildings.

**Garden leave:** This is the kind of enforced, paid leave, stipulated in contracts to stop contractees walking straight from one job into another with 'sensitive information'

**Generica:** What fast food, strip malls and commercial monopolies have done to the 'burbs. You could be anywhere and they'd all look the same!

**Glocalisation:** This is the natural portmanteau word to encompass "Think Global, Act Local". In reality it's just a notion to ease the pain of the small guys going out of business when the chainstore muscles in.

**Guilt-free leave:** Leaving behind laptops, mobile phones etc. when going on holiday leave because it's in the company's policy.

**Gung holier than thou/ Gung holiness:** Might is right. The unswerving belief that one is absolutely morally righteous when armed to the teeth with military hardware.

**Identity theft:** Because of the nature of today's computerised technology, it has become possible to totally steal another's identity e.g. through passport numbers and credit cards, records kept in databases.

**Imprinting:** The sinister belief that kids are like ducklings — get at them early enough and they'll be true to you all their lives!

**Little big spenders:** Those under 16s with the huge bank balances who like to shop till they drop.

**Magalogs:** Mail-order catalogues disguised as real magazines to lull their recipients.

**Manorexia:** This is the male version of the female 'anorexia' —the manifestation is usually less in self-starvation and more in obsessive gym work and compulsive fat calorie counting.

**Market of one:** The business notion that through the power and ubiquity of the Information Superhighway, marketing can be uniquely tailored to the individual consumer's tastes.

**Mouse potato:** The internet generation's version of the 'couch potato'

**Nutraceutical:** Food product that claim some added health benefit e.g. tastes fantastic AND reduces cholesterol)

**Opinion formers:** Thought leaders—be they radio or TV opinion gurus e.g. Oprah Winfrey can influence sales of products making overnight successes or anathema to certain industries e.g. the Texan meat debacle.

**Panic Management:** The fine line trodden by spin doctors when they try to keep populations effectively alert but not alarmed. In the former state they consume more!

**Political equity:** What the big corporations hope they are buying with their very generous donations.

**Presenteeism:** Working long hours (often needlessly) because of either a macho culture, fear for your job and unnatural love of your job or a combination of the three.

**Pushing the envelope**: Reaching the outer limits of the possible — so often used that it is effectively meaningless.

**Quality circles:** The work groups within a company who are supposed to work tirelessly at improving the quality of a product. Is there any ceiling? Are these as mysterious as crop circles?

**Rent-a-quotes:** The willing, media-loving experts who pop up frequently on TV etc. to give their endorsements and testimonials, chosen not because they are the best at what they do but because they understand about sound bites and are well known.

**Sarchasm:** The 'I-don't-get-it' gap between the acidic wit and the clueless audience.

**Snoutcasts:** The nicotine lepers huddled and puffing on footpaths and alleys because of the new Prohibition — Cigarette Free Zone Work Areas.

**Solution:** Like 'quality', solution started out as a perfectly decent word. But unfortunately Corporate jargonese has been feeding frenziedly on its verbal corpse for some decades. Now it has become a bottom feeder as it has become verbified 'solutioning the problem'

**Stepford workers:** Cloned, zombified corporate employees — the corporation has achieved its ultimate objective and turned the company collective into an ant hill with all the worker ants doing exactly what they are bid, unquestioningly.

**Terminal care facility:** Don't be fooled! This is a euphemism for 'retirement home' the kind you buy a one-way ticket for.

**Text pot:** The kind of youthling whose elevated social standing is indicated by the high frequency of their SMS message beeps.

**Text starved:** This is the opposite to the Text Pot, that poor soul whose phone stays conspicuously silent.

**Thought leadership:** The ability to say the blindingly obvious before someone else does.

**Treeware:** This is the IT slang for paper information, hard copy.

**Trend rifts:** this is what they call it when unforeseen trends suddenly explode e.g. massive growth of the Internet.

**Tweenies:** You're a tweenie before your teens. The 8-12 year olds who are seen as rich pickings by companies because they are still malleable.

**Ultraretirement:** What happens when you retire at 55 and die at 100? It's a new phenomenon where the first part is Ultra leisure and the second part is Terminal Care Facility. Who's going to be able to pay for this?

**Upskill:** A way of 'adding value' to yourself as an employee by learning new skills.

**Verbification:** This is the tendency to turn quite acceptable nouns into substandard verbs—e.g. remoting, tasking, incentivising.

**Visioning:** What used to be called forecasting.

**Vulture capitalists:** The kind of predatory companies who circle ailing businesses with a view to stripping them and picking their bones clean.

# CORPORATE CLICHÉS

at the end of the day
back to the drawing board
bottom line is
brave new world
breakthrough
challenges we face
client focused
committed to
competency based
continuous improvement
core values
crafting a mission statement
cutting edge
defining moment
fast forward
focus group
foreseeable future
forward looking
forward planning
fully diversified
fully integrated
get the message across
give 110%
glass ceiling
going forward
head count
heart of the matter
heated argument
holy grail
in regards to
in terms of
in the final analysis
infrastructure
knowledge management
level playing field
margins matter
meaningful dialogue

meeting the challenge
no blame
no pain, no gain
on message
on the back burner
outside the box
paving the way
people are our greatest asset
performance appraisal
plays a role in
pose a threat
push the envelope
put in place
ratcheted up
reach deep inside
re-engineering
rest is history
roll it out
runs on the board
sea change
send a message
seriously consider
serves a role or roll
shareholder value
stakeholder
start the ball rolling
success factors
take-home message is
taking it to the next level
team player
up in the air
value add
viable alternative
walk the talk
win-win situation
world's best practice
your call is important to us

# FLIMFLAM LANGUAGE

*This is the language of doublespeak and deception.*
*Corporations and authorities have maestros of spin*
*devising ways to make*
*actions, directives and stuff-ups 'palatable'*

## MILITARY SPIN

### Invasion
active defence
insertion
liberation
shock and awe

### Killing
collateral damage
dehousing
energetic disasembly
ethnic cleansing
friendly fire
incontinent ordnance
liquidation
mopping up
neutralise
servicing the target
softening up
target of opportunity
wet work

### Bombing
aerial ordnance
laying down a carpet
daisy cutting
MOAB (massive ordnance air blast)
surgical strike

## CORPORATE SPIN

### Firing staff
brightsizing
business process re-engineering
career change opportunity
cashier
decruitment
dehiring
downaging
involuntary career event
jettison employees
non-continuing
offshored
paring down
rightsizing
spill and fill
surplused
tough decisions
uninstalled

### Corporate deceit
accounting irregularity
corporate oversight system
expectation-reality mismatch
massage the figures
plausible deniability
rationalised footprint
restatement of earnings
shifting the goalposts
strategic oversight
structural adjustment
tax avoision
aggressive accounting

# THE PITFALLS OF SPELLING

I take it you already know
Of tough and bough and cough and dough.
Others may stumble, but not you,
On hiccough, thorough, slough and through.
Well done! And now you wish, perhaps,
To learn of less familiar traps?

Beware of heard, a dreadful word,
That looks like beard and sounds like bird.
And dead—it's said like bed, not bead;
For goodness sake, don't call it deed!
Watch out for meat and great and threat.
(They rhyme with suite and straight and debt.)
A moth is not a moth in mother;
Nor both in bother, broth in brother.

And here is not a match for there,
Nor dear and fear for bear and pear;
And then there's dose and rose and lose —
Just look them up — and goose and choose;
And cork and work and card and ward,
And font and front and word and sword.
And do and go, then thwart and cart.
Come, come, I've hardly made a start.

A dreadful language? Why man alive,
I learned to talk it when I was five.

    — *author unknown*

# TICKLED PINK

*Is there any wonder that someone learning English might have trouble understanding our idioms? Observe how many shades of meaning there are alone for colours.*

## BLACK

*In Western countries, black is the colour of mourning.*

*Black has sinister connotations as you can see by some these idioms.*

black and blue — bruised
black and white — clearly distinct or different
blackguard — scoundrel
blackhearted — evil
black humour — rather dark comedy
black market — under the radar economics
black out — lose consciousness
black sheep — outcast
black tie — formal
blackball — to ostracise someone or refuse them entry
blacklist — to ban from entry or membership
blackout — loss of electricity
blackmail — use sensitive material to gain financial ends
the pot calling the kettle black
black sheep — the outcast

## BLUE

*In Iran blue is the colour of mourning.*

*Blue is also used as a protection against witches.*

*A room painted blue is said to be relaxing.*

*The pharaohs wore blue for protection against evil.*

blue — sad
blue blood — royal, regal
bluebook — list of socially prominent people
blue movies — pornographic movies
bluenose — a strictly puritanical person
blueprint — plans for construction or infrastructure

blue ribbon — awarded to the "Best of Show" or competition
bluestocking — the upper class woman
bluestone — grey sandstone used for building
blue-collar workers — manual labour
into the blue — the vast unknown
once in a blue moon — rarely
out of the blue — from nowhere
sing the blues — soulful music
true blue — loyal

## GREEN

*Green is the national colour of Ireland.*
*Green means 'go'*
*Green is for healing, the colour of nature.*
greenback — US dollar bill
green-eyed monster — jealousy
green around the gills — looking pale and seedy.
greenhorn — a newcomer, novice
green light — the go ahead
green room — where guests and performers wait to be called
                        or relax after the show
green with envy — jealous

## PURPLE

*The Egyptian queen Cleopatra loved purple. To obtain one*
*ounce of Tyrian purple dye, she had her servants soak 20,000*
*Purpura snails for 10 days.*

*In Thailand, purple is worn by a widow mourning her*
*husband's death.*

*Purple is considered the colour of royalty.*

*Leonardo da Vinci believed that the power of meditation was*
*increased tenfold when done in a purple light.*

Purple Heart — US military decoration

born to purple —  born into royalty

purple prose — full of exaggerated ornamentation
purple speech — profane talk

# RED

*Because of its high visibility stop signs and danger warnings are all painted red.*

*In South Africa, red is the colour of mourning.*

*In Russia, red means beautiful.*

*In India, red symbolises the military.*

*In China, red is the colour of good luck — it is used in weddings and babies are given their names at a red-egg ceremony.*

in the red — in debt
red-eye — overnight airplane flight
red flag — danger or caution
red herring — a distraction
red hot — the "in" thing
red meat — beef, lamb, pork, kangaroo
red neck — yokel, right-wing
red tape — bureaucracy
red-faced — embarrassed
red-handed — caught in the act
red-letter day — a day of good luck, special importance
roll out the red carpet — VIP treatment
to paint the town red — celebrate
to see red — to be angry

# WHITE

*White flag is the universal truce symbol.*

*White is the colour of mourning in China and Japan.*

*Angels are usually portrayed in white.*

*White is the colour of the traditional wedding dress in Christian cultures.*

white as a sheet — to be very pale
whited sepulchre — a hypocrite, evil inside but appears good
white elephant — an anomaly, something that doesn't fit in

white flag — the universal truce signal
white heat — very hot radiation
white lie — a small fib
white list — contains favoured items
whiteout — loss of visibility in a snow blizzard
white-collar workers — management
whitewash — to gloss over defects
white water — rapids and waterfalls

## YELLOW

*Yellow signifies mourning in Burma and Egypt.*

*In Spain executioners once wore yellow.*

*Yellow is the symbol for a merchant or farmer in India.*

*To holistic healers, yellow signifies peace.*

yellow — cowardly
yellow journalism — irresponsible and alarmist reportage
yellow-belly — coward
yellow ribbon — sign of support for soldiers at the front
yellow streak down one's back — cowardly

# OWE AND EYE

Owe that eye mite bee that be
Winging hur weigh oar the see,
Oar the waives sew bright and blew,
With the fishes glinting threw,
Sea-ing pour-poises at play,
Here-ing the see-hoarses nay,
Passing I-lands green and fare,
With myrrh-mades on them hear and their,
And sumtimes sea a killer whale
Cinque a wore-ship with it's tale.
Owe that eye mite bee as free
Two go winging ore the see!
— *author unknown*

# FLAMBOYANT WORDS  F - P

*More, yes more of these colourful, expressive, ebullient words. Say them out loud, it will make you laugh just to enunciate them.*

**FOIBLE**
Idiosyncratic leaning.

**FOLDEROL**
Trivia or nonsense; a showy but useless item.

**FURBELOW**
Showy ornament or trimmings.

**GADZOOKS**
An exclamation of surprise or annoyance.

**GAZUMP**
Mainly in British or Australian English, to unfairly acquire a property by bidding more than an offer that has already been accepted.

**GOBBLEDYGOOK**
Unintelligible language, especially jargon or bureaucratese.

**GONGOOZLE**
To stare at.

**GOSSOON**
A young lad (could be related to French for boy, 'garçon').

**HABDABS**
A state of extreme nervousness.

**HOBBLEDEHOY**
A clumsy or awkward youth.

**HORNSWOGGLE**
To cheat.  Popeye's refrain every time Brutus diddled him again."I's bin hornswoggled!"

**HUMUNGOUS**
Huge, enormous.

**INFUNDIBULUM**
A funnel-shaped cavity.

**HUGGER - MUGGER**
Clandestine activity, muddle or confusion.

**HULLABALOO**
Uproar or scandal

**HUMDUDGEON**
Imaginary illness.

**INSINUENDO**
Insinuation and innuendo.

**INGLENOOK**
A chimney corner.

**ISHKABIBBLE**
A dismissive statement.

**JACKANAPES**
A cheeky or impertinent person.

**JINGOISM**
Aggressive or warlike patriotism.

**JOBBERNOWL**
A stupid person, a blockhead.

**KATZENJAMMER**
Anxiety or jitters, German for "hangover".

**KERFUFFLE**
A commotion or fuss.

**KLUTZ**
An awkward person.

**LACKADAISICAL**
Lacking enthusiasm and determination; carelessly lazy.

**LANGUESCENT**
Becoming tired.

**LEUCIPOTTOMY**
Cutting white horses onto hillsides.

**LOLLAPALOOZA**
Outstanding.

**LOLLYGAG**
To fool around; to spend time aimlessly; to dawdle or dally.

**MACARONIC**
Containing a mixture of foreign words.

**MALARKEY**
Fooling around, silliness.

**MARITORIOUS**
Being fond of one's husband.

**MIMSY**
Prim or affected; over-refined; mincing.

**MITHRIDATE**
An antidote.

**MOLLYCODDLE**
To treat too protectively.

**MUGWUMP**
Someone who stays aloof.

**MUMBLECRUST**
A toothless one.

**MUNDUNGUS**
Rubbish; refuse.

**NESCIENT**
Ignorant.

**NINNYHAMMER**
Fool or simpleton.

**OOJAH**
A thingumabob, doohickey or whatchamacallit.

**PANDEMONIUM**
Great noise, disorder, confusion.

# WHERE DO YOU STOP?

*The full stop is a punctuation mark to be taken seriously.*
*Its placement gives meaning to words and sentences.*
*Can you put the stops in the right place?*

Mrs Morrissey came into the room on her nose. She had dark glasses on her feet. There were high heels hanging from her ears. She wore her hoop earrings on her fingers. Were lots of gold rings standing there. She looked a kind, happy teacher and we all felt relieved as we smiled. Back at her she walked towards us and shook. Our hands she put a large cloth. Bag on the table and pulled out. A cat then a round ball it was. Then we began to realise that. There was something different. About this teacher we began to wonder. What kind of powers. She had then ...

The letter W is the only letter in the alphabet that doesn't have 1 syllable... it has three.

A hamlet is a village without a church and a town is not a city until it has a cathedral.

"Karate" means "empty hand"

The "v" in the name of a court case doesn't mean versus – it means "and" in civil proceedings or "against" (in criminal proceedings)

"Strengths" is the longest word in the English language with just one vowel.

# COMMONLY MISSPELLED WORDS

absence
accidentally
accommodate
accumulate
achievement
acquaintance
acquire
acquitted
advice
advise
amateur
among
analysis
analyse
annual
apartment
apparatus
apparent
appearance
arctic
arguing
argument
arithmetic
ascend
athletic
attendance
balance
battalion

beginning
belief
believe
beneficial
benefited
boundaries
Britain
business
calendar
candidate
category
cemetery
changeable
changing
choose
chose
coming
commission
committee
comparative
compelled
conceivable
conferred
conscience
conscientious
conscious
control
controversial

controversy
criticise
deferred
definitely
definition
describe
description
desperate
dictionary
dining
disappearance
disappoint
disastrous
discipline
dissatisfied
dormitory
effect
eighth
eligible
eliminate
embarrass
eminent
encouragement
encouraging
environment
equipped
especially
exaggerate

| | | |
|---|---|---|
| excellence | independence | occurrence |
| exhilarate | inevitable | omitted |
| existence | intellectual | opinion |
| existent | intelligence | opportunity |
| experience | interesting | optimistic |
| explanation | irresistible | paid |
| familiar | knowledge | parallel |
| fascinate | laboratory | paralysis |
| February | laid | paralyse |
| fiery | led | particular |
| foreign | lightning | pastime |
| formerly | loneliness | performance |
| forty | lose | permissible |
| fourth | losing | perseverance |
| frantically | maintenance | personal |
| generally | manoeuver | personnel |
| government | manufacture | perspiration |
| grammar | marriage | physical |
| grandeur | mathematics | picnicking |
| grievous | maybe | possession |
| height | mere | possibility |
| heroes | miniature | possible |
| hindrance | mischievous | practically |
| hoping | mysterious | precede |
| humorous | necessary | precedence |
| hypocrisy | Negroes | preference |
| hypocrite | ninety | preferred |
| immediately | noticeable | prejudice |
| incidentally | occasionally | preparation |
| incredible | occurred | prevalent |

| | | |
|---|---|---|
| principal | rhythm | surprise |
| principle | ridiculous | technique |
| privilege | sacrifice | temperamental |
| probably | sacrilegious | tendency |
| procedure | salary | tragedy |
| proceed | schedule | transferring |
| profession | seize | tries |
| professor | sense | truly |
| prominent | separate | tyranny |
| pronunciation | separation | unanimous |
| pursue | sergeant | undoubtedly |
| quantity | severely | unnecessary |
| quizzes | shining | until |
| recede | similar | usually |
| receive | sincerely | village |
| receiving | sophomore | villain |
| recommend | specifically | weather |
| reference | specimen | weird |
| referring | statue | whether |
| repetition | studying | woman |
| restaurant | succeed | women |
| rhyme | succession | writing |

Why do 'overlook' and 'oversee' mean opposite things?

Why is the man who invests all your money called a broker?

If people from Poland are called *Poles*,
why aren't people from Holland called *Holes*?

# GUESSTIMATES!

*Sometimes words suggest a meaning — children are
particularly good at offering suggestions
Alas, many of us, as we age, lose our willingness for silliness !*

| | |
|---|---|
| **Accrostic** | A stick that's lost its temper. |
| **Acoustic** | An instrument used in shooting pool. |
| **Accrue** | People who work on a ship. |
| **Adamant** | The very first insect. |
| **Alarms** | What an octopus is. |
| **Alimony** | The high cost of leaving. |
| **Ambition** | Goaled rush. |
| **Ambivalence** | Two decides to every question. |
| **Antisocial** | Mother's sister being friendly. |
| **Apathy** | Vigor mortis. |
| **Archaeologist** | A man whose career lies in ruins. |
| **Artery** | Study of paintings. |
| **Aspire** | Where dead donkeys are cremated. |
| **Atlas** | Finally! |
| **Atrophy** | An award given to those who do not exercise. |
| **Avail** | Piece of cloth that stops woman from looking so ugly. |
| **Avoidable** | What a bullfighter tries to do. |
| **Bacteria** | The rear entrance to a cafeteria. |
| **Boycott** | His crib...not hers! |
| **Broadband** | An all girl musical group. |
| **Budget** | An attempt to live below your yearnings. |
| **Burglarize** | What a crook sees with. |
| **Cantaloupe** | Got to get married in Church. |
| **Carnation** | Country where everybody has a four wheeler. |
| **Caramel** | A motorised camel. |
| **Cauterise** | Made eye contact with her. |
| **Choosy Blond** | One for whom a Tom or a Harry won't do. |
| **Circumvent** | The opening in the front of boxer shorts. |
| **Cistern** | Opposite of brothern. |
| **Climate** | The only thing you can do with a ladder. |
| **Coffee** | A person who is coughed upon. |

| | |
|---|---|
| **Coincide** | What most people do when it rains. |
| **Control** | A short, ugly inmate. |
| **Continuant** | An ant who just keeps on going. |
| **Counterfeiter** | Worker who puts together kitchen cabinets. |
| **Damnation** | Beaver country. |
| **Dance** | Vertical expression of a horizontal idea. |
| **Dare** | Not here. |
| **Decagon** | De way you explain how your vehicle was a total washout in an accident. |
| **Decay** | De letter which comes after de J. |
| **Depth** | Height turned upside down. |
| **Determine** | Keep men at arm's length. |
| **Dilate** | To live long. |
| **Disguise** | Always chasing dismisses. |
| **Disneyland** | A people trap operated by a mouse. |
| **Dogmatic** | Run by canine power. |
| **Donkey** | Instrument to get you into the godfather's residence. |
| **Eclipse** | What an English barber does for a living. |
| **Economist** | A person who knows more about money than people who have it. |
| **Enema** | Not a friend. |
| **Eyedropper** | A clumsy ophthalmologist. |
| **Fibula** | A small lie. |
| **Fiction** | The story told by a completed Income Tax Form. |
| **Finite** | Sir Lancelot. |
| **Fobia** | The fear of misspelled words. |
| **Forum** | In favour of drinking Bacardi. |
| **Gargoyle** | An olive-flavoured mouthwash. |
| **Golddigger** | A sweet young girl with the gift of the grab. |
| **Hatchet** | What a hen does to an egg. |
| **Heroes** | What a guy in a canoe does. |
| **Humbug** | A singing cockroach. |
| **Illegal** | A sick bird. |
| **Infantry** | A sapling. |
| **Outpatient** | Person who has fainted after seeing a Doctor's bill. |
| **Polarise** | What penguins see with |
| **Polygon** | Who left the cage door open? |

| | |
|---|---|
| **Potash** | All that's left after you have smoked the joint. |
| **Primate** | Removing your spouse from in front of the TV. |
| **Protein** | Favouring young people. |
| **Rampage** | Section of a book about male sheep. |
| **Ratify** | To use a spell and turn a person into a rodent. |
| **Realm** | To be charitable ... once again! |
| **Rebel** | What you have to do when kids don't come to class when first called. |
| **Recount** | Road from Florida to the White House. |
| **Rectangle** | What the fisherman was left with after his brush with Moby Dick. |
| **Rectitude** | The formal, dignified demeanour assumed by a proctologist immediately before he examines you. |
| **Rectum** | It almost killed them. |
| **Reduce** | A messed up point in Tennis, when you were on 'Advantage' |
| **Regatta** | Where the drunkard found himself tonight. again! |
| **Relief** | What trees do in the spring. |
| **Render** | The animals that draw Santa's carriage. |
| **Roman** | What you need to do to win the Regatta. |
| **Rubberneck** | What you can do to relax your wife. |
| **Sauna Bath** | A slimming pool. |
| **Seamstress** | Describes 90 kilos in a size 8. |
| **Selfish** | What the owner of a seafood store does. |
| **Subdued** | A guy that works on submarines. |
| **Terminal** | |
| **Illness** | Sickness at an airport. |
| **Testicle** | A humourous question on an exam. |
| **Treason** | What the acorn is to the oak. |
| **Tumor** | An extra pair. |
| **Urine** | Opposite of "you're out"! |
| **Varicose** | Located nearby. |
| **Wise-crack** | A comedian with a PhD. |
| **Zebra** | Ze cloth which covers ze breasts. |

# JINGLE JANGLE WORDS

*These words are guaranteed to give you a bit of a chuckle.*
*If we can keep these 'echo words' in our vocabulary, we won't*
*get too serious.* **echo words.**

## JANGLY-MANGLEY

| | | |
|---|---|---|
| amber gambler | criss-cross | gender bender |
| argie-bargie | crop top | Georgie Porgie |
| arsey darsey | culture vulture | gibble-gabble |
| arsey-versey | date rape | handstand |
| arty-farty | Delhi belly | hanky-panky |
| arty-tarty | dilly-dally | happy-clappy |
| back pack | ding-dong | harum-scarum |
| Bali belly | dippy-hippy | heebie-jeebies |
| barmy army | double trouble | hey-day |
| bee's knees | dream team | hi fi |
| big wig | drip-drop | higgledy-piggledy |
| blackjack | easy-peasey | hocus pocus |
| blue blood | Evil Knievel | hoity-toity |
| boob tube | fag hag | hokey cokey |
| boogie-woogie | fan-tan | holus bolus |
| boo hoo | fat cat | Hong Kong |
| bow wow | fee fi fo fum | honky tonky |
| boy toy | fender-bender | hootchi-coochi |
| brain drain | fiddle faddle | hotch-potch |
| cheeky chappie | fiff-faff | hot head |
| chiff-chaff | flash-trash | hot pot |
| chip shop | flat tack | how now? |
| chitter-chatter | flim-flam | hubbub |
| clap-trap | flip-flop | hugger-mugger |
| clink-clank | flower power | hullaballoo |
| clip-clop | fun fur | humdrum |
| clitter-clatter | fun run | hunky dorey |
| cop shop | funny bunny | hurdy gurdy |
| cosi cosa | fuzzy wuzzy | hurly-burly |
| creepy-crawly | gee gaw | ill will |

itsy-bitsy
jibber-jabber
jiggery-pokery
jingle-jangle
jim-jams
jump jet
knickerbockers
knick-knack
know how
kowtow
lily-livered
listeria hysteria
lovey-dovey
lubbelly-jubbelly
Mini Minor
mish-mash
mop-chop
mumbo jumbo
namby-pamby
night light
niminy-piminy
nitty gritty
nit wit
no go
noodnik
no show
odd bods
ogle-mogle
okey-dokey
omnium gatherum
party pooper
peg leg
pell-mell
pen pal
picnic
pie-eyed

piggywiggy
pilpul
ping pong
pindy-pandy
pinky-winky
pishery-pashery
pitter-patter
plip-plop
pooper scooper
pot shot
rag bag
raggle-taggle
rat-tat-tat
razzle dazzle
rich bitch
riff-raff
road rage
rumpy-pumpy
shell shock
shilly-shally
ship shape
shock jock
silly billy
Simple Simon
sing-song
skid lid
slapdash
slip-slops
slow coach
snail mail
snicker-snacker
snip-snap
space race
stranger danger
stun gun
superduper

super-trooper
swan song
swing-wing
tank top
teensy-weensy
teeny-weeny
teepee
teeter-totter
tell tale
think tank
tip-toe
tip-top
tittle-tattle
tohu-bohu
toowit toowoo
topsey-turvey
toy boy
traduttore
traditore
tric trac
true blue
tuppenny-ha'penny
upsy-daisy
vice versa
walkie-talkie
whipper-snipper
wibbly-wobbly
wiggle-waggle
wigwam
willy-nilly
wing-ding
wishy-washy
won-ton
yoo hoo
zig-zag

# JINGLE-JINGLES

ack-ack
agar-agar
aye aye
baa baa
bang-bang
Barbar (rugby
club)
beri-beri
bob-bob (defecate)
bon-bon
booboo
bulbul (Persian
bird)
buzz buzz (in
Hamlet )
bye-bye
can-can
cha-cha
chi-chi
chin-chin
choo-choo
chop chop
cocoa
cous cous
tutu
twenty-twenty
two-two

dada
din-din
dodo
dumdum
fifty-fifty
frou-frou
gaga
gee-gee
gilly-gilly
girlie-girlie
go-go
goody goody
haha
ho-ho-ho
housey housey
hush hush
jaw-jaw
jug-jug
ju-ju
knock-knock
Koko (the clown)
lulu
mama
Mau-Mau
wa-wa waw waw
willie-willie
woof-woof

motmot (riverine
bird)
muu muu (shift
dress)
never-never
night-night
no-no (the noun)
papa
paw-paw
peri-peri (small
hot beans)
pip-pip
pocketa-pocketa
pooh pooh
puff-puff
rara
ro-ro
so-so
ta-ta
Tintin
tomtom
tsetse
tusk tusk
tut tut
ylang-ylang

## JINGLES-AND-JANGLES

beck and call
bed and board
bits and bobs
cash and carry
cheap and cheerful
chopping and changing

hither and thither
classes and masses
dribs and drabs
fiddle and faff
flotsam and jetsam
high and dry

## MORE JINGLES AND
## JANGLES

king and country

kiss and cuddle

kith and kin

Marks and Sparks

mix and match

nobs and yobs

odds and sods

pic'n'mix

pitch and put

pongs and gongs

pots and pans

Pride and Prejudice

primp and preen

rough and ready

Sense and Sensibility

smells and bells

so and so

spic and span

stars and stripes

such and such

surf-n-turf

thick and thin

this and that

thrills and spills

to and fro

top and tail

toss and turn

town and gown

Tweedledum and Tweedledee

yin and yang

# BEFUDDLED?

*Judicial / Judicious*
Judicial means relating to judges or legal processes.
Judicious means sound in judgement, prudent.

*Junction / Juncture*
Junction is a point at which one or more things are joined.
Juncture denotes a conjunction of events producing a
dramatic or critical moment.

*Lessee / Lessor*
Lessee is the person who holds the property by lease.
Lessor is the person who lets a property by lease.

# ALPHA BRAVO

*Here is the alphabet of radio communications*
*used by aviators, emergency services, the police and the*
*military. English is the international language of aviation.*
*Reception of radio links is sometimes not clear enough to*
*distinguish between sounds such as*
*B, P, T and V*

A - Alpha
B - Bravo
C - Charlie
D - Delta
E - Echo
F - Foxtrot
G - Gulf
H - Hotel
I - India
J - Juliet
K - Kilo
L - Lima
M - Mike
N - November
O - Oscar
P - Papa
Q - Quebec
R - Romeo
S - Sierra
T - Tango
U - Uniform
V - Victor
W - Whiskey
X - X-ray
Y - Yankee
Z - Zulu

# PROWORDS

*"Prowords" are standard words used
by the military and emergency services to keep radio
communications brief and unambiguous.*

ACKNOWLEDGE — Station acknowledges they have heard the message.

AFFIRMATIVE — Yes, you are correct or what you have transmitted is correct.

ALL AFTER / ALL BEFORE — Used for making repetitions.

CANCEL — Cancel a message or part of a message.

CLOSE DOWN — Stations are to close down when indicated.

CLOSING DOWN — Station is closing down.

CODE X — Confidential message — use headphones.

CORRECTION — An error has been made in transmission. The correct version follows.

FETCH — Used in conjunction with a name or appointment.

FIGURES — Used in difficult conditions before sending figures digit by digit.

GRID — Used before any grid reference.

SAY AGAIN / I SAY AGAIN — Used for repetitions.

I SPELL — Used when spelling out a word.

MESSAGE — Used when message should be written down.

NOTHING HEARD — No signals received from a station.

OUT — This marks the end of the transmission.

OUT TO YOU — This ends the call to you and a call to another station follows immediately.

OVER — This is the end of the transmission to you and a reply is expected.

RADIO CHECK — Report how you receive my transmission.

READ BACK — Repeat the entire transmission back to me exactly as you received it.

RELAY TO — Instruction to a station to relay a message.

ROGER — I have received the last transmission successfully.

SEND — I am ready to receive your message.

VERIFY — Verify portion with originator, send correct version.

WAIT — I must pause for five seconds. Everyone wait.

# FEAR OF... SOMETHING, ANYTHING

A man who fears suffering
is already suffering from what he fears.
*Michel de Montaigne*

*What do we fear? As many things as you can imagine, and
then some. They are called phobias and
here's a SHORT list.*

### A
Alcohol — *Methyphobia.*
Amnesia — *Amnesiphobia.*
Animals — *Zoophobia.*
Ants — *Myrmecophobia.*

### B
Bacteria — *Bacteriophobia.*
Bald people — *Peladophobia.*
Beards —*Pogonophobia.*
Bicycles — *Cyclophobia.*
Birds — *Ornithophobia.*
Black — *Melanophobia.*
Books — *Bibliophobia.*
Bullets — *Ballistophobia.*
Bulls — *Taurophobia.*
Bums or beggars —*Hobophobia.*

### C
Cats — *Aclurophobia.*
Celestial spaces — *Astrophobia.*
Cemeteries — *Coimetrophobia.*
Ceremonies, religious — *Teleophobia.*
Changes, making; moving —*Tropophobia.*
Chickens — *Alektorophobia.*
Children — *Pedophobia.*
Chinese or Chinese culture — *Sinophobia.*
Choking — *Anginophobia.*

Clocks or time — *Chronophobia.*
Clothing — *Vestiphobia.*
Cold or cold things — *Frigophobia.*
Computers or working on computers — *Technophobia.*
Corpses — *Necrophobia.*
Creepy, crawly things — *Herpetophobia.*
Criticism — *Enissophobia.*
Crystals or glass — *Crystallophobia.*

## D

Death or dying — *Thanatophobia.*
Defeat — *Kakorrhaphiophobia.*
Dental surgery — *Odontophobia.*
Dependence on others — *Soteriophobia.*
Depth — *Bathophobia.*
Disorder or untidiness — *Ataxophobia.*
Doctor, going to the — *Iatrophobia.*
Dogs or rabies — *Cynophobia.*
Dolls — *Pediophobia.*
Double vision — *Diplophobia.*
Drinking — *Dipsophobia.*
Drugs, new — *Neopharmaphobia.*
Duty or responsibility, neglecting — *Paralipophobia.*

## E

Eating or swallowing — *Phagophobia.*
Eight, the number — *Octophobia.*
Electricity — *Electrophobia.*
Eyes, opening one's — *Optophobia.*

## F

Failure — *Atychiphobia.*
Fainting — *Asthenophobia.*
Fatigue —*Kopophobia.*
Female genitalia — *Eurotophobia.*
Fever — *Febriphobia.*
Fire — *Pyrophobia.*
Firearms — *Hoplophobia.*

Forgetting or being forgotten — *Athazagoraphobia.*
Freedom — *Eleutherophobia.*
Friday the 13th — *Paraskavedekatriaphobia.*
Frogs — *Batrachophobia.*
Functioning or work: surgeon's fear of operating
— *Ergasiophobia.*
Fur or skins of animals — *Doraphobia.*

### G
Germs — *Verminophobia.*
Gold — *Aurophobia.*
Good news, hearing good news — *Euphobia.*
Gravity — *Barophobia.*

### H
Hair — *Trichopathophobia.*
Heat —*Thermophobia.*
Heights — *Acrophobia.*
Homosexuality or of becoming homosexual — *Homophobia.*
Horses — *Equinophobia.*
Hospitals — *Nosocomephobia.*
Hurricanes and tornadoes — *Lilapsophobia.*
Hypnotised, being or of sleep — *Hypnophobia.*

### I
Ice or frost — *Pagophobia.*
Ideas — *Ideophobia.*
Ignored, being — *Athazagoraphobia.*
Imperfection — *Atelophobia.*
Infection, contamination or dirt — *Molysmophobia.*
Injections — *Trypanophobia.*
Injury — *Traumatophobia.*
Insanity, dealing with — *Lyssophobia.*
Insanity — *Dementophobia.*
Insects — *Entomophobia.*
Itching — *Acarophobia.*

## K

Kidney disease — *Albuminurophobia.*
Kissing — *Philemaphobia.*

## L

Learning — *Sophophobia.*
Left-handed; objects at the left side of the body
— *Sinistrophobia.*
Lightning and thunder — *Brontophobia.*
Loneliness or of being oneself — *Eremophobia.*
Love, falling or being in — *Philophobia.*

## M

Mad, becoming — *Lyssophobia.*
Meat — *Carnophobia.*
Memories — *Mnemophobia.*
Menstruation — *Menophobia.*
Mind — *Psychophobia.*
Mirrors — *Catoptrophobia.*
Money — *Chrometophobia*
Motion or movement — *Kinetophobia*

## N

Night —*Noctiphobia.*
Noise — *Acousticophobia.*
Number 8 — *Octophobia.*
Number 13 — *Triskadekaphobia.*
Numbers — *Numerophobia.*

## O

Odours or smells — *Olfactophobia.*
Operation, surgical — *Tomophobia.*
Opinions — *Allodoxaphobia.*

## P

People — *Anthropophobia.*
Pins and needles — *Belonephobia.*
Pins — *Enetophobia.*

Place: locked in an enclosed place — *Cleithrophobia.*
Plants — *Botanophobia.*
Pleasure, feeling — *Hedonophobia.*
Poison — *Iophobia.*
Praise, receiving — *Doxophobia.*
Prostitutes or venereal disease — *Cypridophobia*
Puppets — *Pupaphobia.*
Purple, colour — *Porphyrophobia.*

## R
Razors — *Xyrophobia.*
Rat, great mole — *Zemmiphobia.*
Relatives — *Syngenesophobia.*
Religious ceremonies — *Teleophobia.*
Reptiles — *Herpetophobia.*
Responsibility or duty, neglecting — *Paralipophobia.*
Ruin — *Atephobia.*
Running water — *Potamophobia.*

## S
Sacred things or priests — *Hierophobia.*
School — *Scolionophobia.*
Self, seeing oneself in a mirror — *Eisoptrophobia.*
Self, being oneself — *Autophobia.*
Sermons — *Homilophobia.*
Shadows — *Sciophobia.*
Sharks — *Selachophobia.*
Shellfish — *Ostraconophobia.*
Shock — *Hormephobia.*
Sin — *Hamartophobia.*
Single, staying single — *Anuptaphobia.*
Sinning — *Peccatophobia.*
Skin lesions — *Dermatophobia.*
Sleep — *Somniphobia.*
Snakes — *Ophidiophobia*
Social (fear of being evaluated negatively in social situations)
— *Social Phobia.*
Solitude — *Monophobia.*

Sounds — *Acousticophobia.*
Spaces, confined — *Claustrophobia.*
Speed — *Tachophobia.*
Spiders — *Arachnephobia*
Stared at, being — *Ophthalmophobia.*
Stars — *Astrophobia.*
Stooping — *Kyphophobia.*
Strangers or foreigners — *Xenophobia.*
Streets — *Agyrophobia.*
String — *Linonophobia.*
Storm, thunder — *Brontophobia.*
Stuttering — *Psellismophobia.*

## T

Tapeworms — *Taeniophobia.*
Technology — *Technophobia.*
Thinking — *Phronemophobia.*
Thunder — *Ceraunophobia.*
Time or clocks — *Chronophobia.*
Toads — *Bufonophobia.*
Trees — *Dendrophobia.*
Trembling — *Tremophobia.*

## U

Ugliness — *Cacophobia.*
Undressing in front of someone — *Dishabillophobia.*
Urine or urinating — *Urophobia.*

## V

Voices or noises, speaking aloud or telephones
— *Phonophobia.*
Voids or empty spaces — *Kenophobia.*
Vomiting — *Emetophobia.*

## W

Waits, long — *Macrophobia.*
Washing — *Ablutophobia.*
Weakness — *Asthenophobia.*

Wealth — *Plutophobia.*
Weight, gaining — *Obesophobia.*
Wine — *Oenophobia.*
Women — *Gynephobia.*
Words — *Verbophobia.*
Words, long — *Hippopotomonstrosesquippedaliophobia.*
Work — *Ergophobia.*
Worms — *Scoleciphobia.*
Wrinkles, getting — *Rhytiphobia.*
Writing — *Graphophobia.*

**X**

X-rays or radiation — *Radiophobia.*

**Y**

Yellow colour — *Xanthophobia.*

---

It's somewhat ironic that the word for 'fear of long words' is, itself such a long one:

**Hippopotomonstrosequippeddaliophobia**

Try letting your analyst know what ails you!

---

# BEFUDDLED?

*Baluster / Bannister*
Baluster means a pillar supporting a rail around a gallery or terrace.
Banister is a single post supporting a handrail to a staircase.

*Breach / Breech*
Breach means break either as a verb or noun.
Breech means the back or lower part of something.

*Biannual / Biennial*
Biannual means twice yearly.
Biannual means every two years.

# HORIBL MES

The European Commission has just announced an agreement whereby English will be the official language of the European Union rather than German, which was the other possibility. As part of the negotiations, Her Majesty's Government conceded that English spelling had some room for improvement and has accepted a 5-year phase-in plan that would be known as *Euro-English*.

In the first year, 's' will replace the soft 'c'  Sertainly, this will make the sivil servants jump with joy. The hard 'c' will be dropped in favor of the 'k'  This should klear up konfusion and keyboards kan have one less letter.

There will be growing publik enthusiasm in the sekond year when the troublesome 'ph' will be replased with the 'f'  This will make words like 'fotograf' 20% shorter!

In the 3rd year, publik akseptanse of the new spelling kan be expected to reach the stage where more komplikated changes are possible. Governments will enkorage the removal of double leters which have always ben a deterent to akurate speling. Also, al wil agre that the horible mes of the silent 'e' in the languag is disgrasful and it should go away.

By the 4th year, peopl wil be reseptiv to steps such as replasing 'th' with 'z' and 'w' wiz 'v'  During ze fifz year ze unesesary 'o' kan be dropd from vords kontaining 'ou' and similar changes vud of kurs be aplid to ozer kombinations of leters. After ze fifz yer ve vil hav a rali sensibl ritn styl. Zer vil be no mor trubl or difikultis and evriun vil find it ezi tu undrstand ech ozer.

Zen Z Drem Vil Finali Kum Tru!!

— *author unknown*

# PORTMANTEAUX

*Coined by Lewis Carroll in "Alice Through the Looking Glass"*
*when he has Humpty Dumpty say:*
*"Well, slithy means lithe and slimy. You see it's like a*
*portmanteau — there are two meanings packed up into*
*one word."*

*Portmanteau (plural portmanteaux) is French for suitcase. It's*
*a way of blending portions of two words to make a new word,*
*and combining their meaning.*

**Affluenza:** affluence + influenza
**Alphabet:** alpha + beta
**Anacronym:** anachronism + acronym
**Anecdata:** anecdote + data
**Animatronics:** animation + electronics
**Artivist:** art + activist
**Automagic:** automatic + magic
**Avionics:** aviation + electronics
**Backronym:** back + acronym
**Blaxploitation:** black + exploitation
**Bacne:** back + acne
**Boxercise:** boxing + exercise
**Brunch:** breakfast + lunch
**Buffeteria:** buffet + cafeteria
**Cafetorium:** cafeteria + auditorium
**Californication:** California + fornication
**Camcorder:** camera + recorder
**Caplet:** capsule + tablet
**Carboloy:** carbon + alloy
**Chillaxing:** chilling out + relaxing
**Chortle:** chuckle + snort (coined by Lewis Carroll)
**Chunnel:** Channel + tunnel
**Cocacolonisation:** Coca-Cola + colonisation

**Cryptex:** cryptology + codex
**Cyborg:** cybernetic + organism
**Digipeater:** digital + repeater
**Discotheque:** disc + bibliotheque
**Dragula:** dragster + dracula
**Dramedy:** drama + comedy
**Dramastic:** dramatic + drastic
**Ebonics:** ebony + phonics
**Faction:** fact + fiction
**Fantabulous:** fantastic + fabulous
**Fanzine:** fan + magazine
**Feminazi:** feminist + nazi
**Finglisi:** Farsi (Persian for "Persian") + Inglisi (Persian for "English")
**Foon:** fork + spoon
**Franglais:** français (French for "French") + anglais (French for "English")
**Gaydar:** gay + radar
**Ginormous:** gigantic + enormous
**Godness:** goddess + goodness
**Guesstimate:** guess + estimate
**Ghettro:** ghetto + retro
**Gymnatorium:** gymnasium + auditorium
**Hairagami:** origami + hair
**Hasbian:** has-been + lesbian
**Hugantic:** huge + gigantic
**Ignoranus:** ignoramus + anus
**Infomercial:** information + commercial
**Janglish:** Japanese + English
**Jazzercise:** jazz + exercise
**Knork:** knife + fork
**Lupper:** lunch + supper
**Manorexic:** man + anorexic

**Manssiere:** man + brassiere

**Mantastic:** man + fantastic

**McJob:** McDonalds + job

**Mechatronics:** mechanics + electronics

**Meld:** melt + weld

**Metrosexual:** most commonly: metropolitan + heterosexual

**Mexifornia:** Mexico + California

**Mimbo:** male + bimbo

**Mingy:** mean + stingy

**Mobisode:** mobile (phone) + episode

**Mockney:** mock + Cockney

**Moped:** motor + pedal

**Motel:** motor + hotel

**Mutagen:** mutation + genesis

**Oxbridge:** Oxford + Cambridge

**Petrochemical:** petroleum + chemical

**Phoneme:** phonetics + scheme

**Pictionary:** picture + dictionary

**Plucot:** plum + apricot

**Pomato:** potato + tomato

**Pretendo:** pretend + Nintendo

**Prosumer:** professional + consumer

**Ridonkulous:** ridiculous + donkey

**Robocop:** robotic + cop

**Rolodex:** rolling + index

**Screenager:** screen (as in a computer monitor) + teenager

**Sexcellent:** sex + excellent

**Sexercise:** sex + exercise

**Sexploitation:** sex + exploitation

**Shemale:** she + male

**Sexplosion:** sexual + explosion
**Simulcast:** simultaneous + broadcast
**Silastic:** silicone + plastic
**Skort:** skirt + short (as in short pants)
**Smaze:** smoke + haze
**Smog:** smoke + fog
**Spork:** spoon + fork
**Sportscast:** sports + broadcast
**Stagflation:** stagnation + inflation
**Swaption:** swap + option
**Tangelo:** tangerine + pomelo
**Teensploitation:** teen + exploitation
**Televangelist:** television + evangelist
**Texican:** Texan + Mexican
**Thermistor:** thermal + resistor
**Transistor:** transfer + resistor
**Truggy:** truck + buggy
**Twigloo:** twig + igloo
**Vanbulance:** van + ambulance
**Wonderosity:** wonder + curiosity
**Wonkavator:** Wonka + elevator

---

Why isn't 11 pronounced onety-one?

Why is a person who plays the piano called a pianist, but a person who drives a race car not called a racist?

If a pig loses its voice, is it disgruntled?

---

# PLURALS 'R' US

We'll begin with a box and the plural is boxes,
But the plural of ox should be oxen, not oxes.

The one fowl is a goose but two are called geese
Yet the plural of moose should never be meese.

You may find a lone mouse or a whole set of mice
Yet the plural of house is houses not hice.

If the plural of man is always called men
Why shouldn't the plural of pan be called pen?

If I speak of a foot and you show me your feet
And I gave you a boot, would a pair be called beet?

If one is a tooth and a whole set is teeth,
Why should not the plural of booth be called beeth?

Then one may be that, and three would be those
Yet hat in the plural wouldn't be hose,
And the plural of cat is cats and not cose.

We speak of a brother and also of brethren,
But though we say mother, we never say methren.

Then the masculine pronouns are he, his and him,
But imagine the feminine, she, shis and shim.

So English I fancy you all will agree
Is the funniest language you ever did see.

— *author unknown*

# ENGILSH ODRER

Aoccdrnig to a rscheearch at an Elingsh uinervtisy, it deosn't mttaer in waht oredr the ltteers in a wrod are, the olny iprmoetnt tihng is taht frist and lsat ltteer is at the rghit pclae. The rset can be a toatl mses and you can sitll raed it wouthit a porbelm. Tihs is bcuseae we do not raed ervey lteter by it slef but the wrod as a wlohe. Ceehiro

According to a researcher at Cambridge University, it doesn't matter in what order the letters in a word are, the only important thing is that the first and last letter be in the right place. The rest can be a total mess and you can still read it without problem. This is because the human mind does not read every letter by itself but the word as a whole.

# MIRROR WRITING

Leonardo da Vinci wrote in small notebooks using his left-hand and a technique of mirror writing (text is written from right to left)   He frequently painted using his left-hand and only ever seemed to write with his right hand when he intended the text to be read easily by others. The mirror script makes Leonardo's work on any topic very difficult to read, plus he made use of unusual spellings and abbreviations, and arranged his notes in no logical order.

Several reasons have been put forward for the use of mirror writing:

He was left-handed and in those days of writing with pen and ink this was a particular disadvantage; as your hand crossed the page it would smudge the still-wet text. Leonardo would have solved this problem with his technique of mirror writing.

He may have been concerned about others stealing his ideas, though mirror writing seems a less than effective form of security.

Leonardo's ideas disagreed with the teachings of the Roman Catholic Church. In particular, he discounted the idea of the Great Flood and the forming of the Earth. Again this assumes he was using mirror script as a form of security.

In the age of Leonardo, people were naturally superstitious and children were normally forced to write using their right hand, so it is unusual to find someone from this period who was so openly a south-paw. When it comes to painting and drawing, Leonardo initially seems to have been ambidextrous, using whichever hand was most convenient. He gradually changed over to almost exclusively using his left hand. Leonardo's left-handedness has assisted greatly in identifying drawings which may be his. A right-handed artist instinctively shades with the lines going from the right down to the left, but a left-handed artist reverses this process.This can be clearly seen in Leonardo's *Portrait of an Unknown Woman.*

If writers write, how come fingers don't fing.
If the plural of tooth is teeth
Shouldn't the plural of phone booth be phone beeth
If the teacher taught,
Why didn't the preacher praught.

If a vegetarian eats vegetables —
What the heck does a humanitarian eat?
Why do people recite at a play
Yet play at a recital?
Park on driveways and drive on parkways

You have to marvel at the unique lunacy
Of a language where a house can burn up
as it burns down,
And in which you fill in a form by filling it out
And a bell is only heard once it goes!

—*author unknown*

# LANGUAGE TRIVIA

"Devil's Advocate" originates from the Catholic Church. When deciding if someone should gain sainthood, a devil's advocate is always appointed to give the opposing view.

William Dampier, the buccaneer explorer who was the first Englishman to discover Australia, coined thousands of words in his travels, one thousand of which are still listed in the Oxford dictionary. Examples are avocado, barbecue and sea lion.

The "D" in D-day means "Day"  The French term for "D-Day" is "J-jour"

There is a word in the English language with only one vowel which occurs six times: Indivisibility.

"lb" the abbreviation for pound, is from the astrological sign Libra, meaning balance and is symbolised by scales.

The word "pixel" is a contraction of either "picture cell" or "picture element".

The word "modem" is a contraction of the words "modulate, demodulate" (MOdulateDEModulate).

"Stewardesses" and "reverberated" are the two longest words (12 letters each) that can be typed using only the left hand.

One of the longest English words which can be typed using the top row of a typewriter (allowing multiple uses of letters) is "typewriter".

# HERE LIES ...

*An epitaph is generally a few lines written to commemorate someone who's died, often found on their tombstone.*

**On a hanged man:**
Rab McBeth
Who died for the want
of another breath.
1791-1823

---

Here lies the body of
Thomas Kemp.
Who lived by wool
and died by hemp.
**Bletchley, England.**

---

**Winterborn Steepleton
Cemetery, Dorsetshire:**
Here lies the body
Of Margaret Bent
She kicked up her heels
And away she went.

---

Here lies old Rastus Sominy
Died a-eating hominy
In 1859 anno domini
**Savannah, Georgia.**

---

He got a fish-bone
in his throat
and then he sang
an angel note.
**Schenectady, New York.**

---

**Rebecca Freeland 1741**
She drank good ale,
good punch and wine
And lived to the age of 99.

---

Beneath this stone,
a lump of clay,
Lies stingy Jimmy Wyatt.
Who died one morning
just at ten
And saved a dinner by it.

---

1690
Here lie the bones of
Joseph Jones
Who ate while he was able.
But once overfed,
he dropt down dead
And fell beneath the table.
When from the tomb,
to meet his doom,
He arises amidst sinners.
Since he must dwell in
heaven or hell,
Take him—whichever gives
the best dinners.

---

Here lies Johnny Cole.
Who died upon my soul
After eating a plentiful dinner.
While chewing his crust. He was turned into dust
With his crimes undigested — poor sinner.

### In memory of Anna Hopewell:

Here lies the body of our
Anna
Done to death by a banana
It wasn't the fruit that laid
her low
But the skin of the thing
that made her go.

---

Enosburg Falls, Vermont:
Here lies cut down like
unripe fruit,
The wife of
Deacon Amos Shute:
She died of drinking too
much coffee,
Anny Dominy
—eighteen-forty.

---

### Roxbury, Connecticut:

Eliza, Sorrowing
Rears This Marble Slab
To Her Dear John
Who Died of Eating Crab.

---

### On a Farmer's Daughter,

Letitia:
Grim Death
To Please His Palate
Has Taken My Lettice
To Put in His Sallat.
**Ipswich.**

### On a gravedigger:

Hooray my brave boys
Lets rejoice at his fall.
For if he had lived
He would have buried us all.

---

Robert Phillip, gravedigger:
Here I lie at the
Chancel door;
Here lie I because I am poor;
The farther in
the more you pay;
Here I lie as warm as they.
**Kingsbridge, England.**

### On a coroner who hanged himself:

He lived
And died
By suicide.
**West Grimstead, Sussex, England.**

---

### On Ezekiel Pease:

Pease is not here,
Only his pod
He shelled out his Peas
And went to his God.
**Nantucket, Massachusetts.**

---

### On a Coal miner:

Gone Underground
For Good.

---

### On a brewer:

G. Winch, the brewer, lies buried here.
In life he was both hale and stout.
Death brought him to his bitter bier.
Now in heaven he hops about.

**On an Architect:**
Here lies Robert Trollope
Who made yon stones roll up.
When death took his soul up
His body filled this hole up.

**On a lawyer in England:**
Sir John Strange.
Here lies an honest lawyer.
And that is Strange.

**On an attorney:**
Goembel John E.
1867-1946
"The defense rests"

**On a dentist:**
Stranger tread
This ground with gravity.
Dentist Brown
Is filling his last cavity.
**Edinburgh, Scotland.**

**On a Painter:**
A Finished Artist.

On an Auctioneer:
Jedediah Goodwin
Auctioneer
Born 1828
Going!
Going!!
Gone!!!
1876.

**On a traveling salesman:**
My Trip is Ended:
Send My Samples Home.
**Hoboken.**

**On a waiter:**
Here lies the body of
Detlof Swenson.
Waiter.
God finally caught his eye.
April 10, 1902.

**On an Author:**
He Has Written Finis.

**On a teacher:**
Professor S. B. McCracken
School is out
Teacher
Has gone home.
**Elkhart, Indiana.**

**On John Yeast:**
Here lies
Johnny Yeast.
Pardon me
For not rising.
**Ruidoso, New Mexico.**

**On John Penny:**
Reader if cash thou are
In want of any
Dig 4 feet deep
And thou wilt find a Penny.
**Wimborne, England.**

**Epitaph on a huge boulder
on the grave of a doctor:**
William P. Rothwell, M.D.
1866-1939
This is on me.
**Oak Grove Cemetery,
Pawtucket,
Rhode Island.**

**On a fisherman:**
Captain Thomas Coffin
Died 1842, age 50 years.
He's done a-catching cod
And gone to meet his God.
**New Shoreham,
Rhode Island.**

**On a gardener:**
To the Green Memory of
William Hawkings
Gardener:
Planted Here
With Love and Care
By His
Grieving Colleagues.
**Davenport.**

**On a housewife:**
Mary Weary, Housewife
Dere Friends I am going
Where washing ain't done
Or cooking or sewing:
Don't mourn for me now
Or weep for me never:
For I go to do nothing
Forever and ever!
**Belchertown.**

Barnard Lightfoot
Who was accidentally killed
in the 45th year of his age.
This monument was erected
by his grateful family.

Here lies the body of
Thomas Vernon
The only surviving son of
Admiral Vernon.
**Plymouth, Mass.**

1787 - Jones - 1855
Here lie the bones of
Sophie Jones;
For her death held no
terrors.
She was born a maid and
died a maid.
No hits, no runs,
and no heirs.
**Scranton, Pennsylvania.**

**Ann Mann**
Here lies Ann Mann,
Who lived an old maid
But died an old Mann.
December 8, 1767
**London, England.**

Sacred to the memory of
Major James Brush
Royal Artillery,
who was killed by the accidental discharge of
a pistol by his orderly,
14th April 1831.
Well done, good and faithful servant.

# NOMS DE WORDS

*A word coined from someone's name is termed an eponym. There are around 35,000 eponyms in the English language. Here are some examples:*

**Axel, figure skating jump** — Axel Paulsen (1855-1938) was a Norwegian figure skater.

**Barbie doll** — Barbara, daughter of Ruth Handler, creator of Barbie.

**Bedlam** — St Mary of Bethlehem was an asylum for the insane in London. It was shortened to "bedlam".

**Biro** — Láslo Biro (1900-85), Hungarian journalist.

**Bloomers** — Amelia Bloomer (1818-94), US women's right campaigner.

**Bougainvillea** — Louis Antoine de Bougainville (1729-1811) French explorer who discovered this plant.

**Boycott** — Captain Charles Cunningham Boycott (1832-1897) was a land agent in Ireland for Earl Eme. He had evicted tenants from their crofts because they couldn't pay the rent. In 1880, the Irish Land League found a non-violent way of retaliating. It was advised that everyone ostracise him and have no dealings with him. It didn't take long for the papers to circulate the story and his name, and the rest, me dears, is history!

**Bunsen burner** — R. W. Bunsen (1811-99), German chemistry professor.

**Busking** — Frederic M. Busk, (1898-1957), US Music Hall and street entertainer.

**Canard** — Jean-Paul Canard (1844-1927), French illusionist.

**Celsius** — Anders Celsius (1701-1744) Swedish astronomer.

**Chauvinism** — Nicolas Chauvin de Rochefort, French soldier. He was apparently an ardent follower of Napoleon Bonaparte and was wounded many times in military campaigns. His colleagues ridiculed him for his slavish devotion to France and their leader. Chauvinism means fanatical patriotism.

**Daguerrotype** — Louis Jacques Mande Daguerre (1787-1851) French artist and chemist.

**Dahlia** — Anders Dahl, (1751-87) Swedish botanist.

**Decibel** — Alexander Graham Bell (1847-1922) inventor of the telephone.

**Diesel** — Rudolf Diesel (1858-1913) inventor of the diesel engine.

**Doberman, dog breed** — Ludwig Doberman, German dog breeder.

**Doozy** — expensive classy make of automobile designed in the late 1920s by Fred Duesenberg (1876-1932).

**Eustachian tube, in ear** — Bartolomeo Eustachi (1500 - 1574) Italian anatomist.

**Fahrenheit** — Gabriel Fahrenheit (1686-1736) German physicist.

**Fallopian tube** — Gabriele Fallopio (1523-1962) Italian physician.

**Frangipani** — Muzio Frangipani, 16 c. Italian Marquis.

**Frisbee** — Mrs Frisbie's Pie tins were used by US college students in the 1930s for throwing around as a game.

**Fuchsia** — Leonard Fuchs (1501-1566).

**Gardenia** — Alexander Garden (1730-1791) American physician and naturalist.

**Gerrymander** — Eldridge Gerry (1744-1814) An American politician who in 1810, whilst Governor of Massachusetts, sought to rearrange the electoral boundaries in favour of his own party. It is told that Gilbert Stuart, the artist, visited the Boston Sentinel newspaper and seeing the newly drawn-up boundaries, proceeded to draw the head, wings and tail of a salamander. Editor Benjamin Russell dubbed it a "gerrymander" and thus the word was born.

**Granny Smith apple** — Maria Ann Smith (1799-1870) was an Australian woman who found these apples growing as a mutation in her orchard.

**Guillotine** — Dr Joseph Ignatz Guillotin (1738-1814) who advocated the use of this decapitation machine.

**Hooligan** — perhaps after Patrick Hooligan, an Irish hoodlum in London around 1898. It is said that Pat and his family attracted a gang of rowdy followers who based themselves at the Lamb and Flag, a public house in South London.

**Jacquard** — J M Jacquard (1757-1834) French inventor, industrialist.

**Jacuzzi** — Candido Jacuzzi (1903-86), Italian/US inventor and businessman.

**Jeep** — originally the GP (meaning 'general purpose').

**Leotards** — Jules Leotard (1842-70), French trapeze artist.

**Luddite** — after Ned Ludd, an English labourer who destroyed labour-saving stocking frames at his textile factory work place around 1779. The word Luddite was adopted in 1811 by a group of workers who destroyed new textile machinery in the Midlands and North of England because they feared job losses. The agitators were subsequently transported or hanged.

**Lutz, figure skating jump** — Alois Lutz (1898-1918) Austrian figure skater.

**Mausoleum** — Mausollus, a Persian satrap whose wife commissioned a huge tomb for him.

**Maverick** — Samuel A. Maverick (1803–70), US cattle-raiser and politician.

**Ockham's Razor** — William of Ockham (1285-1349), English philosopher. Ockham's razor is a theorem that states "Entities are not to be multiplied unnecessarily" Even though it is attributed to this man, no evidence has been found in his writings of these exact words. In effect his theorem claims that general terms or concepts have no existence separate from individual things denoted by the terms.

**Pander** — Pandarus, procurer for Troillus and Cressida.

**Pap smear** — George Papanicolau (1883-1962), Greek/US physician.

**Pavlova** — Anna Pavlova, Russian prima ballerina.

**Poinsettia** — Joel Roberts Poinsett (1779-1851).

**Ponzi scheme, kind of scam** — Charles Ponzi (1877-1949).

**Pyrrhic** — Pyrrhus, c318-272 BC, king of Epirus who won a battle over the Romans however it was costly that he stated: "One more such victory and we are lost".

**Quisling** — Vidkun Quisling (1887-1945) a Norwegian traitor.

**Rolls-Royce** — Charles Rolls and Henry Royce.

**Sadism** — Maquis de Sade, Count Donatien Alphonse Françoise (1740-1814) French writer who depicted sexual perversions in his works. He was imprisoned for many years because of his sexual offences and spent the last part of his life in a mental asylum.

**Salmonella** — Daniel E. Salmon (1850-1914), American veterinarian.

**Sandwich** — John Montagu, 4th Earl of Sandwich, who liked to eat his nibblies between two slices of bread as he played cards.

**Saxophone** — Adolphe Sax (1814–94), Belgian musical-instrument maker.

**Sideburns** — General Ambrose Burnside had distinctive whiskers.

**Teddy bear** — Theodore Roosevelt (1858-1919) American President. On a hunting trip in 1902 he refused to shoot a bear cub. The episode was recorded in the Washington Post with a cartoon. An enterprising shopkeeper cashed in on the story and thus the 'teddy bear' was born.

**Wellington boot** — Arthur Wellesley, 1st Duke of Wellington (1769-1852), British soldier and statesman. The boots were named in his honour and he wore them at his millitary campaigns.

# WONDERS OF SPEECH

Most babies, by the time they are five or six months old, *babble*—that is, they utter sequences of alternating consonants and vowels such as "ba-ba-ba"  Even deaf babies babble. And babies of all nationalities make the same babbling sounds.  Researchers believe that children naturally make all the sounds of all human languages!

As a general rule, a baby utters its first word about 18 months after it is born.

By the time it is two the baby has a vocabulary of about fifty words.

By three the total has jumped to about a thousand.

At six the total is about 13,000 words, and by 18 the now adult will have a comprehension vocabulary of 60,000 words.

On average women say 7,000 words per day. Men manage just over 2,000.

There are more than 2,700 languages in the world. In addition, there are more than 7,000 dialects. A dialect is a regional variety of a language that has a different pronunciation, vocabulary, or meaning.

The most difficult language to learn is Basque, which is spoken in northwestern Spain and southwestern France. It is not related to any other language in the world. It has an extremely complicated word structure and vocabulary.

There are more than 1,000 different languages spoken on the African continent — more than a third of all the world's languages.

# ET TU, BRUTE?

*If you've ever wondered at the parting words of some of our more famous, erudite or infamous, here are a few offerings.*

**Et tu Brute?**
Stabbed to death by a group of senators led by Brutus.
Roman Emperor, Gaius Julius Caesar, d. 44 BC

**Is it not meningitis?**
Louisa M. Alcott, writer, d. 1888

**Am I dying or is this my birthday?**
When she woke briefly during her last illness and found all her family around her bedside.
Lady Nancy Astor, d. 1964

**Nothing, but death.**
When asked by her sister, Cassandra, if there was anything she wanted.
Jane Austen, writer, d. July 18, 1817

**How were the receipts today at Madison Square Garden?**
P. T. Barnum, entrepreneur, d. 1891

**Is everybody happy? I want everybody to be happy. I know I'm happy.**
Ethel Barrymore, actress, d. June 18, 1959

**Die? I should say not, dear fellow. No Barrymore would allow such a conventional thing to happen to him.**
John Barrymore, actor, d. May 29, 1942

**Now comes the mystery.**
Henry Ward Beecher, evangelist, d. March 8, 1887

**Friends applaud, the comedy is finished.**
Ludwig van Beethoven, composer, d. March 26, 1827

**I should never have switched from Scotch to Martinis.**
Humphrey Bogart, actor, d. January 14, 1957

**Oh, I am not going to die, am I? He will not separate us, we have been so happy.**

Spoken to her husband of 9 months, Rev. Arthur Nicholls.
Charlotte Bronte, writer, d. March 31, 1855

**Beautiful.**
In reply to her husband who had asked how she felt.
Elizabeth Barrett Browning, writer, d. June 28, 1861

**Now I shall go to sleep. Goodnight.**
Lord George Byron, writer, d. 1824

**I am still alive!**
Stabbed to death by his own guards — (as reported by Roman
historian Tacitus) Gaius Caligula, Roman Emperor, d.41 AD

**Don't let poor Nelly (his mistress, Nell Gwynne) starve.**
Charles II, King of England and Scotland, d. 1685

**That was the best ice-cream soda I ever tasted.**
Lou Costello, comedian, d. March 3, 1959

**Goodnight my darlings, I'll see you tomorrow.**
Noel Coward, writer, d. 1973

**Damn it ... Don't you dare ask God to help me.**
To her housekeeper, who had begun to pray aloud.
Joan Crawford, actress, d. May 10, 1977

**That was a great game of golf, fellers.**
Harry Lillis "Bing" Crosby, singer / actor, d. October 14, 1977

**I am not the least afraid to die.**
Charles Darwin, d. April 19, 1882

**I must go in, the fog is rising.**
Emily Dickinson, poet, d. 1886

**Adieu, mes amis. Je vais à la gloire.**
**(Farewell, my friends! I go to glory!)**
Isadora Duncan, dancer, d. 1927

**It is very beautiful over there.**
Thomas Alva Edison, inventor, d. October 18, 1931

**No, I shall not give in. I shall go on. I shall work to the end.**
Edward VII, King of Britain, d. 1910

**All my possessions for a moment of time.**
Elizabeth I, Queen of England, d. 1603

**I've never felt better.**
Douglas Fairbanks, Sr., actor, d. December 12, 1939

**I've had a hell of a lot of fun and I've enjoyed every minute of it.**
Errol Flynn, actor, d. October 14, 1959

**A dying man can do nothing easy.**
Benjamin Franklin, statesman, d. April 17, 1790

**Yes, it's tough, but not as tough as doing comedy.**
When asked if he thought dying was tough.
Edmund Gwenn, actor, d. September 6, 1959

**God will pardon me, that's his line of work.**
Heinrich Heine, poet, d. February 15, 1856

**Turn up the lights, I don't want to go home in the dark.**
O. Henry (William Sidney Porter), writer, d. June 4, 1910

**I am about to take my last voyage, a great leap in the dark.**
Thomas Hobbes, writer, d. 1679

**I see black light.**
Victor Hugo, writer, d. May 22, 1885

**Father, into thy hands I commend my spirit.**
From Luke 23:46
Jesus Christ

**Does nobody understand?**
James Joyce, writer, d. 194

**Now I have finished with all earthly business, and high time too. Yes, yes, my dear child, now comes death.**
Franz Leher, composer, d. October 24, 1948

**Why do you weep. Did you think I was immortal?**
Louis XIV, King of France, d. 1715

**I am a Queen, but I have not the power to move my arms.**
Louise, Queen of Prussia, d. 1820

**Too late for fruit, too soon for flowers.**
Walter De La Mare, writer, d. 1956

**Let's cool it brothers ...**
Spoken to his assassins, 3 men who shot him 16 times.
Malcolm X, Black leader, d. 1966

**Go on, get out — last words are for fools who haven't said enough.**
To his housekeeper, who urged him to tell her his last words so she could write them down for posterity.
Karl Marx, revolutionary, d. 1883

**Nothing matters. Nothing matters.**
Louis B. Mayer, film producer, d. October 29, 1957

**It's all been very interesting.**
Lady Mary Wortley Montagu, writer, d. 1762

**I knew it. I knew it. Born in a hotel room — and God damn it — died in a hotel room.**
Eugene O'Neill, writer, d. November 27, 1953

**Get my swan costume ready.**
Anna Pavlova, ballerina, d. 1931

**I love you Sarah. For all eternity, I love you.**
Spoken to his wife.
James K. Polk, US President, d. 1849

**I owe much; I have nothing; the rest I leave to the poor.**
François Rabelais, writer, d. 1553

**Put out the light.**
Theodore Roosevelt, US President, d. 1919

**Sister, you're trying to keep me alive as an old curiosity, but I'm done, I'm finished, I'm going to die.**
Spoken to his nurse.
George Bernard Shaw, playwright, d. November 2, 1950

**They couldn't hit an elephant at this dist ...**
Killed in  battle during the US Civil War.
General John Sedgwick, Union Commander, d. 1864

**I've had eighteen straight whiskies, I think that's the record.**
Dylan Thomas, poet, d. 1953

**Woe is me. Methinks I'm turning into a god.**
Vespasian, Roman Emperor, d. 79 AD

**I have offended God and mankind because my work did not reach the quality it should have.**
Leonardo da Vinci, artist, d. 1519

**I die hard but am not afraid to go.**
George Washington, US President, d. December 14, 1799

**Go away. I'm all right.**
H. G. Wells, novelist, d. 1946

**Either that wallpaper goes, or I do.**
Oscar Wilde, writer, d. November 30, 1900

**Curtain! Fast music! Light! Ready for the last finale! Great! The show looks good, the show looks good!**
Florenz Ziegfeld, showman, d. July 22, 1932

**I can't sleep.**
James M. Barrie, author, d. 1937

Outside of a dog, a book is man's best friend.
Inside of a dog it's too dark to read.

— *Groucho Marx*
*(1890 - 1977)*

# DESCRIPTIVE ADJECTIVES

*This is a book about words and language so why not a little glossary of adjectives to describe certain linguistic traits?*

APHORISTIC: containing short, pithy statements
BILINGUAL: fluent in two languages
COLLOQUIAL: casual, familiar language use
CRASSILINGUAL: thick-tongued
EFFABLE : able to be expressed
EUPHONIOUS: well-sounding
FACETIOUS: light-footed, cheeky wit
FUSTIAN: pompous, inflated
GARRULOUS: talkative
GINGIVAL: pronounced at the top of the tongue near gum
GLIB: smooth talker
GRANDILOQUENT: pompous or boastful language
GUTTURAL: articulated in the back of the throat
HIGHFALUTIN' : pertaining to pretentious language
LACONIC: using few words, economic use of spoken words
LEXICURIOUS: being curious about language
LINGUISHED: skilled in languages
LOGOFASCINATED: fascinated by words
MALACOPHONOUS: having a soft voice
MELODIOUS: having a pleasing voice
MONOGLOT: fluent in only one language
PAUCILOQUENT: using the fewest words possible to make
    your point
POLYGLOT: multilingual
SESQUIPEDALIAN: using very long words
SURD: voiceless, unvoiced
SYNTACTIC: pertaining to syntax
TAUTEGORICAL: saying the same thing with different words
TITULAR: existing in name or title only
TRALATITIOUS: metaphorical
VERNACULAR: belonging to one's own native land
VOLITIVE: pertaining to a wish or permission

# TO BEGIN AT THE BEGINNING ...

*Many an avid reader would state categorically that the test of a "great book" is its very first lines. Do they grab you? Do they make you want to read on?*

*Well take a look at these for openers.*

To begin at the beginning: It is spring, a moonless night in the small town, starless and bible-black.
*Under Milk Wood*, Dylan Thomas

To see a world in a grain of sand,
And a heaven in a wild flower,
Hold infinity in the palm of your hand,
And eternity in an hour.
*Auguries of Innocence*, William Blake

It was a bright cold day in April, and the clocks were striking thirteen. Winston Smith, his chin nuzzled into his breast in an effort to escape the vile wind, slipped quickly through the glass doors of Victory Mansions, though not quickly enough to prevent a swirl of gritty dust from entering along with him.
*1984*, George Orwell

My father's family name being Pirrip, and my Christian name Philip, my infant tongue could make of both names nothing longer or more explicit than Pip.
*Great Expectations*, Charles Dickens

What can you say about a twenty-five-year-old girl who died? That she was beautiful and brilliant? That she loved Mozart and Bach, the Beatles, and me?
*Love Story*, Erich Segal

In my younger and more vulnerable years my father gave me some advice that I've been turning over in my mind ever since. "Whenever you feel like criticising anyone," he told me, "just remember that all the people in this world haven't had the advantages that you've had.

*The Great Gatsby*, F. Scott Fitzgerald When Mary

Lennox was sent to Misselthwaite Manor to live with her uncle, everybody said she was the most disagreeable-looking child ever seen.

*The Secret Garden,* Frances Hodgson Burnett

My heart aches, and a drowsy numbness pains my sense.
*Ode to a Nightingale,* John Keats,

1801.—
I have just returned from a visit to my landlord — the solitary neighbour that I shall be troubled with.
*Wuthering Heights,* Emily Bronte

All happy families are alike; each unhappy family is unhappy in its own way.
*Anna Karenina,* Leo Tolstoy

A throng of bearded men, in sad-colored garments and gray, steeple-crowned hats, intermixed with women, some wearing hoods, and others bareheaded, was assembled in front of a wooden edifice, the door of which was heavily timbered with oak.
*The Scarlet Letter* by Nathaniel Hawthorne

It was the best of times, it was the worst of times, it was the age of wisdom, it was the age of foolishness, it was the epoch of belief, it was the epoch of incredulity, it was the season of Light, it was the season of Darkness, it was the spring of hope, it was the winter of despair, we had everything before us, we had nothing before us, we were all going direct to Heaven, we were all going direct the other way - in short, the period was so far like the present period, that some of its noisiest authorities insisted on its being received, for good or for evil, in the superlative degree of comparison only.
*A Tale of Two Cities,* Charles Dickens

Many years later, as he faced the firing squad, Colonel Aureliano Buendia was to remember that distant afternoon when his father took him to discover ice.
*One Hundred Years of Solitude,* Gabriel Garcia Marquez

Robert Cohn was once middleweight boxing champion of Princeton. Do not think that I am very much impressed by this as a boxing title, but it meant a lot to Cohn.
*The Sun Also Rises,* Ernest Hemingway

Alice was beginning to get very tired of sitting by her sister on the bank, and of having nothing to do: once or twice she had peeped into the book her sister was reading, but it had no pictures or conversations in it, 'and what is the use of a book,' thought Alice 'without pictures or conversation?'
*Alice's Adventures in Wonderland,* Lewis Carroll

Mr. Sherlock Holmes, who was usually very late in the mornings, save upon those not infrequent occasions when he was up all night, was seated at the breakfast table.
*The Hound of the Baskervilles,* Sir Arthur Conan Doyle

Once, when I was six years old I saw a beautiful picture in a book about the primeval forest called *True Stories.* It showed a boa constrictor swallowing an animal. Here is a copy of the drawing.
*The Little Prince,* Antoine de Saint-Exupery

If you really want to hear about it, the first thing you'll probably want to know is where I was born, and what my lousy childhood was like, and how my parents were occupied and all before they had me, and all that David Copperfield kind of crap, but.
*The Catcher in the Rye* by J.D. Salinger

Squire Trelawney, Doctor Livesey, and the rest of these gentlemen having asked me to write down the whole particulars about Treasure Island, from the beginning to the end, keeping nothing back but the bearings of the island, and that only because there is still treasure not yet lifted, I take up my pen in the year of grace 17 — and go back to the time when my father kept the Admiral Benbow Inn, and the brown old seaman, with the sabre-cut, first took up his lodging under our roof.
*Treasure Island,* Robert Louis Stevenson

I returned from the City about three o'clock on that May afternoon pretty well disgusted with life.
*The Thirty-Nine Steps*, John Buchan

The drought had lasted now for ten million years, and the reign of the terrible lizards had long since ended.
*2001: A Space Odyssey*, Arthur C. Clarke

Mr Jones, of the Manor Farm, had locked the hen-houses for the night, but was too drunk to remember to shut the pop-holes.
*Animal farm*, George Orwell

There was no possibility of taking a walk that day.
*Jane Eyre*, Charlotte Bronte

Whether I shall turn out to be the hero of my own life, or whether that station will be held by anybody else, these pages must show.
*David Copperfield*, Charles Dickens

A squat grey building of only thirty-four storeys. Over the main entrance the words, CENTRAL LONDON HATCHERY AND CONDITIONING CENTRE, and, in a shield, the World State's motto, COMMUNITY, IDENTITY, STABILITY.
*Brave New World*, Aldous Huxley

All children, except one, grow up.
*Peter Pan*, J.M. Barrie

It is a truth universally acknowledged, that a single man in possession of a good fortune must be in want of a wife.
*Pride and Prejudice*, Jane Austen

Emma Woodhouse, handsome, clever, and rich, with a comfortable home and happy disposition, seemed to unite some of the best blessings of existence; and had lived nearly twenty-one years in the world with very little to distress or vex her.
*Emma*, Jane Austen

Christmas won't be Christmas without any presents,' grumbled Jo, lying on the rug.
*Little Women*, Louisa May Alcott

In a certain village in La Mancha, which I do not wish to name, there lived not long ago a gentleman — one of those who have always a lance in the rack, an ancient shield, a lean hack and a greyhound for coursing.
*Don Quixote*, Miguel de Cervantes Saavedra

He lay on the brown, pine-needled floor of the forest, his chin on his folded arms, and high overhead the wind blew in the tops of the pine trees.
*For Whom the Bell Tolls*, Ernest Hemingway

Far out in the uncharted backwaters of the unfashionable end of the Western Spiral arm of the Galaxy lies a small, unregarded yellow sun.
*The Hitchhiker's Guide to the Galaxy*, Douglas Adams

Stately, plump Buck Mulligan came from the stair head, bearing a bowl of lather on which a mirror and a razor lay crossed.
*Ulysses*, James Joyce

On an exceptionally hot evening early in July a young man came out of the garret in which he lodged in S. Place and walked slowly, as though in hesitation, towards K. Bridge.
*Crime and Punishment*, Fyodor Dostoyevsky

It was a pleasure to burn.
*Fahrenheit 451*, Ray Bradbury,

Dr Iannis had enjoyed a satisfactory day in which none of his patients had died or got any worse.
*Corelli's Mandolin*, Louis de Bernières

The studio was filled with the rich odour of roses, and when the light summer wind stirred amidst the trees of the garden, there came through the open door the heavy scent of the lilac, or the more delicate perfume of the pink-flowering thorn.
*The Picture of Dorian Gray*, Oscar Wilde

If I should die, think only this of me: That there's some corner of a foreign field That is forever England.
*The Soldier*, Rupert Brooke

Midway in our life's journey, I went astray from the straight road and woke to find myself alone in a dark wood.
*The Divine Comedy, Inferno,* Dante Alighieri

I was born in the Year 1632, in the City of York, of a good Family, tho' not of that Country, my Father being a Foreigner of Bremen, who settled first at Hull,
*Robinson Crusoe*, Daniel Defoe

Last night I dreamt I went to Mandalay again.
*Rebecca*, Daphne du Maurier

James Bond, with two double bourbons inside him, sat in the final departure lounge of Miami Airport and thought about life and death.
*Goldfinger*, Ian Fleming

Achilles' cursed anger sing, O goddess, that son of Peleus, which stated a myriad sufferings for the Achaeans.
*The Iliad*, Homer

When Farmer Oak smiled, the corners of his mouth spread till they were within an unimportant distance of his ears, his eyes were reduced to chinks, and diverging wrinkles appeared round them, extending upon his countenance like the rays in a rudimentary sketch of the rising sun.
*Far from the Madding Crowd*, Thomas Hardy

It was love at first sight. The first time Yossarian saw the chaplain he fell madly in love with him.
*Catch-22*, Joseph Heller

It is this day three hundred and forty-eight years six months and nineteen days that the good people of Paris were awakened by a grand pealing from all the bells in the three districts of the Cité, the Université, and the Ville.
*The Hunchback of Notre-Dame,* Victor Hugo

As Gregor Samsa awoke one morning from uneasy dreams he found himself transformed in his bed into a gigantic insect.
*The Metamorphosis,* Franz Kafka

Mr. and Mrs. Dursley, of Number Four, Privet Drive, were proud to say that they were perfectly normal, thank you very much. They were the last people you'd expect to be involved in anything strange or mysterious, because they just didn't hold with such nonsense.

*Harry Potter and the Philosopher's Stone,* J.K. Rowling

Call me Ishmael.

*Moby Dick,* Herman Melville

Once there were four children whose names were Peter, Susan, Edmund and Lucy. This story is about something that happened to them when they were sent away from London during the war because of the air-raids.

*The Lion, the Witch and the Wardrobe,* C.S. Lewis

It was a queer, sultry summer, the summer they electrocuted the Rosenbergs, and I didn't know what I was doing in New York.

*The Bell Jar,* Sylvia Plath

Of man's first disobedience, and the fruit of that forbidden tree, whose mortal taste brought death into the world, and all our woe, with loss of Eden.

*Paradise Lost,* John Milton

Here is Edward Bear, coming downstairs now, bump, bump, bump, on the back of his head, behind Christopher Robin.

*Winnie the Pooh,* A.A. Milne

On they went, singing 'Eternal Memory', and whenever they stopped, the sound of their feet, the horses and the gusts of wind seemed to carry on their singing.

*Doctor Zhivago,* Boris Pasternak

I began this disorderly and almost endless collection of scattered thoughts and observations in order to gratify a good mother who knows how to think.

*Emile,* Jean-Jacques Rousseau

You will rejoice to hear that no disaster has accompanied the commencement of an enterprise which you have regarded with such evil forebodings.

    *Frankenstein,* Mary Wollstonecraft Shelley

In a hole in the ground there lived a hobbit. Not a nasty, dirty, wet hole, filled with the ends of worms and an oozy smell, nor yet a dry, bare, sandy hole with nothing in it to sit down on or to eat: it was a hobbit-hole, and that means comfort.

    *The Hobbit,*
    J.R.R. Tolkien (John Ronald Reuel Tolkien)

The Nellie, a cruising yawl, swung to her anchor without a flutter of the sails, and was at rest.

    *Heart of Darkness,* Joseph Conrad

When shall we three meet again
In thunder, lightning, or in rain?

    *Macbeth,* William Shakespeare

Renowned curator Jacques Sauniere staggered through the vaulted archway of the museum's Grand Gallery.

    *The Da Vinci Code,* Dan Brown

---

Some editors are failed writers,
but so are most writers.
*T. S. Eliot*

You don't write because you want to say something,
you write because you have something to say.
*F Scott Fitzgerald,* 1945

What I like in a good author is not what he says,
but what he whispers.
*Logan Pearsell Smith,* 1933

# ENGLISH - A POT POURRI

*Linguistic multiculturalism!*

**Afrikaans**
apartheid, commando, slim, trek.

**Algonquin**
caribou, racoon, tomahawk.

**Arabic**
alcohol, calibre, monsoon, zero.

**Basque**
anchovy, bizarre, jingo.

**Bengali**
bungalow, dinghy.

**Breton**
carol, gaberdine, garrotte, valet.

**Cantonese**
chopsuey, lychee, wok.

**Catalan**
capsize, paella.

**Cornish**
bludgeon, gull.

**Croatian**
cravat.

**Czech**
pistol, polka, robot.

**Dutch**
boss, cookie, lottery, yacht.

**Egyptian**
ammonia, ebony, ivory, paper.

**Farsi**
checkmate, lemon, shawl, tambourine.

**Finnish**
sauna.

**Flemish**
brick, duffle, gas, hunk.

**French**
ambulance, diplomat, parachute, sauce.

**German**
blitz, dollar, muffin, quartz.

**Greek**
athlete, democracy, metropolis, museum.

**Hebrew**
amen, gauze, kosher, messiah.

**Hindi**
bangle, jungle, shampoo.

**Hungarian**
coach, goulash, paprika, sabre.

**Icelandic**
eider, geyser, saga.

**Inuit**
anorak, husky, igloo, kayak.

**Italian**
bankrupt, fascist, opera, umbrella.

**Japanese**
judo, karate, soy, tycoon.

**Korean**
hangul, kimchi, tae kwon do.

**Latvian**
sleazy.
**Lithuanian**
eland, sable.
**Malay**
amok, bamboo, gong,
orang-utan.
**Mandarin**
kowtow, kung fu, typhoon.
**Maori**
haka, kiwi.
**Maya**
cigar, shark.
**Norse**
berserk, husband,
reindeer, window.
**Norwegian**
fjord, iceberg, ski, walrus.
**Phoenician**
gypsum, purple.
**Polish**
horde, mazurka.
**Portuguese**
breeze, flamingo,
marmalade, molasses.
**Romany**
cosh, gigolo, pal.
**Russian**
bistro, cosmonaut,
mammoth, vodka.
**Sanskrit**
candy, orange, sugar.

**Swedish**
boulder, mink,
smorgasbord, Tungsten.
**Swiss French**
chalet, glacier, moraine.
**Swiss German**
bivouac, muesli.
**Syriac**
abbot, damson, Mammon.
**Tagalog**
boondocks, yo-yo.
**Tahitian**
tattoo.
**Tamil**
anaconda, curry, mango,
pariah.
**Thai**
Siamese.
**Tibetan**
lama, sherpa, yak, yeti.
**Turkish**
caviar, kebab, tulip,
yoghurt.
**Ukrainian**
balaclava, Cossack.
**Urdu**
purdah.
**Walloon French**
rabbit.
**Welsh**
corgi, maggot, penguin.
**Yiddish**
bagel, glitch, nosh.

# CARPE DIEM!

*Seize the day! Latin, a so-called dead language, has left a huge legacy in our vernacular. Apart from the roots of many words, not to mention prefixes and suffixes, here are some terms that survive to this day. Much is kept alive by the legal profession, which may be a wise move, as Latin is more impressive.*

**a posteriori:** later, following.

**a priori:** based on theory rather than observation.

**ad absurdum:** to absurdity

**ad extremum:** at last

**ad hoc:** toward this (matter): something created especially for a particular occasion

**ad hominem:** to the man; an argument that relies on personal attacks rather than reason

**ad infinitum:** to infinity, without limit

**ad interim:** for the meantime

**ad nauseam:** to feel disgust; to go on endlessly

**alter ego:** a second self

**anno domini:** year of the lord

**annus mirabilis:** miraculous year

**argumentum ab ignorantiam:** arguing from ignorance

**bona fide:** in good faith, genuine

**carpe diem:** seize the day

**casus belli:** an act justifying war

**caveat emptor:** let the buyer beware

**cum grano salis:** with a grain of salt

**corpus delicti:** the body of the crime

**cum gratia:** with the approval of

**de facto:** in fact; something that is automatically accepted, though not officially recognised

**Deo volente (d.v.):** God willing

**ecce homo:** behold the man

**ergo:** therefore; used to show a logical conclusion

**et alia (et.al.)** and others

**et cetera:** and so forth

**ex cathedra:** with written authority

**ex libris:** from the library of

**ex mea sententia:** in my opinion

**ex officio :** by virtue of an official capacity

**ex post facto:** after the deed

**exempli gratia (e.g.):** for example

**flagrante delicto:** caught in the act

**fortuna suffragante:** with luck on our side

**habeus corpus:** a writ forcing authorities to bring a person trial/court or release him

**humum mandere:** to bite the dust

**ibidem (ibid) :** the same book/ person/ source

**id est (i.e.):** that is

**Ignotum per ignotius:** A thing unknown by a thing more unknown (used to describe something in terms that are even less understandable)

**in camera:** in secret

**in absentia:** in one's absence

**in culpa versari:** to be at fault

**in memoriam:** in memory of

**in posterum:** till the next day

**in quaestione versare:** to be under investigation

**in loco parentis :** in the place of a parent

**in toto:** entirely

**in vino veritas:** wine makes people speak the truth

**inter alia:** among other things

**ipso facto:** it speaks for itself, by the fact itself

**locum tenens :** a stand-in for a professional colleague

**me fallit:** I do not know

**mirabile dictu:** marvellous to behold

**modus operandi:** a method of working

**multis post annis:** many years later

**mutatis mutandum :** with the necessary changes

**ne plus ultra:** the most intense quality or state, no peer

**nihil ad rem:** irrevelant

**non sequitur:** does not logically follow

**non compos mentis:** not of sound mind

**nota bene:** take note, observe well

**Pax vobiscum:** peace to you.

**per annum:** yearly

**per capita:** for each person, per head

**per diem:** by the day

**per se:** by itself; essentially

**persona non grata:** unwelcome person

**post mortem:** after death

**pro forma:** carried out as a formality

**pro patria:** for one's country

**pro rata:** in proportion

**quidnunc:** one who is curious to know everything, gossip

**quid pro quo:** something for something

**quod erat demonstrandum:** that which has been proved

**quod vide (q.v.):** what will be seen

**sic:** thus, as written

**sine die:** indefinitely, without a date

**sine qua non:** a necessity

**sui generis:** unique

**tempus fugit :** time flies

**terra incognita:** unknown world, territory

**vox populi:** voice of the people, poll

# WISE LATIN SAYINGS

Nosce te ipsum.

*Know thyself.*

Minima maxima sunt.

*The smallest things are most important.*

Ubi dubium, ibi libertas.

*Where there is doubt, there is freedom.*

Non illegitimus carborundum.

*Don't let the bastards get you down!*

Errate humanum est.

*To err is human.*

# FRANGLAIS

*Little wonder that English has a plethora of French words and phrases - the language was literally dominated by French after the Norman Conquest for hundreds of years.*
*Here's a soupçon.*

**amour propre:** pride in oneself, not wanting to lose face

**au naturel:** unseasoned, naked, unadorned

**au pair:** a person who works for a family in exchange for board

**avant garde:** innovative, out there

**bête noire:** pet peeve

**billet doux:** love letter

**bon appétit:** enjoy your meal!

**bon vivant:** someone who knows how to live it up

**bon voyage:** have a good trip

**c'est la vie:** that's life!

**fait accompli:** a done deed

**carte blanche**: a free hand, open slather

**chargé d'affaires:** in charge of business

**comme il faut:** as it should be done

**coup de grace:** final blow

**coup d'état:** overthrow the government

**crème de la crème:** cream of the crop

**cul-de-sac:** dead end street

**décolletage:** low neckline

**déjà vu:** feeling that you have already experienced something before

**demitasse:** half a glass

**de rigueur:** culturally obligatory

**double entendre:** a word play, double meaning

**enfant terrible:** wild, unruly person

**fait accompli:** a done deed

**faux pas:** a foolish mistake or foot in mouth

**femme fatale:** a deadly woman, alluring myterious

**fin de siècle:** end of the century or an era

**folie à deux:** a craziness that takes over two people at same time – often those in love suffer from this condition

**haute couture:** high fashion

**hors de combat:** out of action

**je ne sais quoi:** unable to put my finger on it

**mot juste:** exactly the right word or expression

**nom de plume:** pen name

**papier maché:** mashed paper – an art form

**par excellence:** the best of the best

**pièce de résistance:** outstanding accomplishment

**raison d'être:** justification for existing

**rendez-vous:** appointment

**sang froid:** maintain your composure

**savoir faire:** tact or social grace, nouse

**soupçon:** a hint, the merest bit

**tête-à-tête:** a private talk

**tour de force:** requiring a great deal to accomplish

**trompe l'oeil:** tricks the eye – a painting style which makes you believe that it's real

**vol-au-vent:** very light pastry pockets

# PARROT FASHION

*The following article, "Parrot's oratory stuns scientists",
appeared in an online BBC article by Alex Kirby, 24 January,
2004. It describes the extraordinary linguistic talents of a bird
called N'kisi.*

The finding of a parrot with an almost unparalleled power to
communicate with people has brought scientists up short.

The bird, a captive African grey called N'kisi, has a
vocabulary of 950 words, and shows signs of a sense of
humour.

He invents his own words and phrases if he is confronted
with novel ideas with which his existing repertoire cannot
cope — just as a human child would do...

About 100 words are needed for half of all reading in English,
so if N'kisi could read he would be able to cope with a wide
range of material.

He uses words in context, with past, present and future
tenses, and is often inventive.

One N'kisi-ism was "flied" for "flew", and another "pretty
smell medicine" to describe the aromatherapy oils used by his
owner, an artist based in New York.

When he first met Dr Jane Goodall, the renowned
chimpanzee expert, after seeing her in a picture with apes,
N'kisi said: "Got a chimp?"

He appears to fancy himself as a humourist. When another
parrot hung upside down from its perch, he commented:

"You got to put this bird on the camera."

Dr Goodall says N'kisi's verbal fireworks are an "outstanding example of interspecies communication"

In an experiment, the bird and his owner were put in separate rooms and filmed as the artist opened random envelopes containing picture cards.

Analysis showed the parrot had used appropriate keywords three times more often than would be likely by chance.

---

*When is the singular more than its plural?*

Hair is a singular word that suggests more than its plural, hairs.

*Fish or fishes?* When you are referring to a group of fish of the same species they are called fish, but once you refer to several species they are called fishes.

*The plural words:*

adventures, bras, cares, cites, cosines, deadlines, esquires, marques, millionaires, multimillionaires, ogres, prelates, princes, saltines, shines, sightlines, squires, tartines, timelines

*all become different singular words if you add another 's' onto the end of each.*

*Many of them switch from masculine plural form to feminine singular form.*

---

# TRICKS FOR REMEMBERING

*Mnemonics (pronounced with the first 'm' silent) is the art of using acronyms or phrases or sentences based on initials of lists or groups to remember those items.*

**Planetary order (remember that Pluto no longer a planet!): Mercury, Venus, Earth, Mars, Jupiter, Saturn, Uranus, Neptune**

*My Very Efficient Monkey Just Sorted Unused Napkins*

*My Very Elegant Mother Just Served Us Nachos*

*More vitally effective Measures Could Just Save Us Now.*

**Planetary order with the inclusion of the three dwarf planets: Mercury, Venus, Earth, Mars, Jupiter, Saturn, Uranus, Neptune, Ceres, Pluto, Xena**

*My Very Eccentric Mother Could Just Send Us Nineteen Cheerleaders Playing Xylophones*

**For remembering the new "dwarf planets" Xena , Ceres and Pluto.**

*X-rays Cure People.*

*Xavier Can Punctuate.*

**Turning screw threads: left Anti-clockwise, Right clockwise** *Lefty, loosey — Righty, tighty*

**Metric Lengths:**

| kilo | hecto | deca | meter | deci | centi | milli |
|------|-------|------|-------|------|-------|-------|
| x1000 | x100 | x10 | 1 | 1/10th | 1/100th | 1/1000th |
| Km | Hm | Dm | m | dm | cm | mm |

*Killer Hound Dog Meets Deadly Cat Man*

**Addressing people of letters:** Mr. J.Smith, V.C., M.A. and Roy Jones, Esq., D.S.O., B.Sc., M.P.
*Honour before degree, Degree before M.P.*

**Parts of speech:** Pronoun, Adverb, Noun, Conjunction, Adjective, Preposition, Interjection, Verb.
*The sailor's favourite boat was named PAN CAP IV*

**First Aid Priorities Reminder—Danger, Response, Airway, Breathing. Circulation — DRABC**

**Signs of the Zodiac:** Aries, Taurus, Gemini, Cancer, Leo, Virgo, Libra, Scorpio, Sagittarius, Capricorn, Aquarius, Pisces.
*A Tense Grey Cat Lay Very Low, Sneaking Slowly, Contemplating A Pounce*

**Brain lobes**
*" First Place Often Takes the Trophy."*
*(Frontal, Parietal, Occipital, Temporal, Temporal)*
The temporal lobe has two hemispheres.
**Treatment of Insect Stings**
*"Use Ammonia for a Bee sting,*
*and Vinegar for a Wasp sting"*
*(A is followed by B, and V by W)*

To remember the difference between **affect** vs **effect**
RAVEN
*Remember Affect Verb Effect Noun*

**How to spell geography**
*Gordon eats old greasy rabbits and plants his yams.*
*George eats old gray rats and paints houses yellow.*
*George Ellen's Old Grandmother Rode A Pig Home Yesterday*

**Remembering two s's in dessert**
*Would you rather have one S or two? Twice as much for dessert. When you eat dessert, you always want to come back for the second 's'*

**For remembering Lichen is made up of Algae and Fungi**
She was *all gal* (ALGAL) and he was a *fun guy* (FUNGI)
They took a *likin'* (LICHEN) to each other

## Days in each month
*30 days hath September,*
*April, June and November,*
*All the rest have 31,*
*Excepting February alone*
*(And that has 28 days clear,*
*With 29 in each leap year)*

## Difference between Principle and PrinciPAL
Your principal is your *PAL*

## For remembering: Kingdom, Phylum, Class, Order, Family, Genus, Species
*Kings Play Cards On Fat Girls' Stomachs*
*Kids Prefer Cheese Over Fried Green Spinach*
*King Phillip Came Over From Greece Sailing Vessels*
*Kittens Prefer Cream Or Fish, Generally Speaking*

## Spelling NECESSARY:
**1 c, 2 s's.** *One collar, two socks*

## Remembering what happened to Henry VIII's six wives
***D****ivorced,* ***B****eheaded,* ***D****ied,* ***D****ivorced,* ***B****eheaded,* *Survived*

## To practice typing every letter of the alphabet
*The quick brown fox jumps over the lazy dog*

## For the order of the bones in the wrist: Scaphoid, Lunate, Triquetral, Pisiform, Trapezium, Trapezoid, Capitate, Hamate
***S****ome* ***L****overs* ***T****ry* ***P****ositions* ***T****hat* ***T****hey* ***C****an't* ***H****andle*

## Latitude and longitude
***Long****-itude is the distance ALONG the Equator from Greenwich (in degrees) and*
***Lat****-itude is the lateral (or up and down) distance North/ South from the Equator (in degrees)*

## The world's longest rivers
*" NAM-MI  YACH-Y!"*
*Nile (Africa) - 4,145 miles*
*Amazon (S.America) - 4,050 miles*
*Mississippi-Missouri (USA) - 3,760 miles*
*Irtysh (Russia) - 3,200 miles*
*Yangtse (China) - 3,100 miles*
*Amur (Asia) - 2,900 miles*
*Congo (Africa) - 2,718 miles*

## First Men to Visit the Moon
*A - B - C*

*Neil Armstrong, Buzz Aldrin, Michael Collins*

## For remembering the Vitamins and their uses:

*Vitamin A*
*Keeps the cold germs away*
*and tends to make meek people nervy.*
*B's what you need*
*when you're going to seed*
*and C is specific in scurvy.*
*Vitamin D*
*makes the bones in your knee*
*tough and hard for the service on Sunday,*
*while E makes hens scratch*
*and increases the hatch*
*and brings in more profits on Monday.*
*Vitamin F never bothers the chef*
*for the vitamin never existed,*
*G puts the fight*
*in the old appetite and you eat all the foods that are listed.*

*So now when you dine, remember each line*
*If long on this globe you will tarry:*
*Just try to be good and pick out more food*
*From the orchard, the garden and dairy.*

**The Plagues of Egypt**
*"Retaliating For Long Frustration, MOSES Badgered Hostile Leader Demanding Freedom" being: River to blood, Frogs, Lice, Flies, Murrain (ie.foot-&-mouth disease), Boils, Hail, Locusts, Darkness, First-born.*

**Continents — Europe, Antarctica, Asia, Africa, Australia, N.America, S.America**
*Eat An Aspirin After A Nutella Sandwich*

**For remembering how to spell RHYTHM**
*Rythm Helps Your Two Hips Move.*

# BEFUDDLED?

*Medal / Meddle /Metal / Mettle*
Medal means 'a small flat piece of inscribed metal'
Meddle means 'to interfere in another's affairs'
Metal means 'any of a number of classes of elements which are solid and lustrous.'
Mettle means courage, spirit.'

*Scrimp / Skimp*
Scrimp used in context of 'scrimp and save.' To work hard.
Skimp means 'to be sparing or frugal.'

*Turbid / Turgid*
Turbid means 'muddy or hazy/'
Turgid means 'pompous, bombastic.'

# FLAMBOYANT WORDS  P- Z

*More words to make you smile and roll around on your tongue for the sheer delight of it. Try taking them for a test run from time to time. Slide one or two into your day-to-day and see if it doesn't brighten your life and that of others.*

## PANJANDRUM
A mock title for a person, real or imaginary, who has or, claims to have, great influence or authority.

## PARAPHERNALIA
Miscellaneous articles or personal possessions.

## PECCADILLO
A minor indiscretion.

## PEDUNCLE
A stalk- like appendage in a biological organism.

## PETARD
A small explosive charge.

## PICAYUNE
Trifling, paltry.

## POPINJAY
A vain or conceited person, one given to pretentious displays.

## PSITHURISM
Low whispering sound, such as leaves rustling.

## PUCKEROO
Useless, broken.

## PUSILLANIMOUS
Timid, faint-hearted.

## PYKNIC
Short and fat.

## QUIDNUNC
A newsmonger or gossip.

**QUISQUILLIOUS**
Trashy, worthless.

**RAMBUNCTIOUS**
Lively, hard to control.

**RIGMAROLE**
A lengthy and complicated procedure.

**RHINOTILLEXOMANIA**
Habitual or obsessive nose-picking.

**SARCOPHAGUS**
A stone coffin, typically adorned with a sculpture or
inscription.

**SERENDIPITY**
The ability to make unexpected and fortunate discoveries.

**SESQUIPEDALIAN**
Relating to long words.

**SHEMOZZLE**
A brawl, scene of confusion or chaos.

**SHENANIGANS**
Boisterous high spirits.

**SILLABUB**
A dessert made mostly from cream.

**SKEDADDLE**
Scram, disappear fast.

**SKULDUGGERY**
Dirty work. Can mean they're up to no good.

**SNICKERSNEE**
A large knife.

**SNOLLYGOSTER**
A shrewd unprincipled person.

**SPONDULICKS**
Money, cash.

**TATTERDEMALION**
A tattered or ragged person.

**TERMAGANT**
A harsh-tempered or overbearing woman.

**THIBLE**
A spatula.

**THIGMOTAXIS**
An animal's movement brought on by a mechanical device.

**TINTINNABULATION**
A ringing or tinkling sound.

**TOHUBOHU**
A state of chaos, confusion.

**TUMULTUOUS**
Disorderly, rowdy, restless.

**TWADDLE**
Utter rubbish in speaking or writing.

**UMBLES**
Entrails of an animal.

**UNGULATA**
The zoological order of hoofed animals.

**VEXILLOLOGY**
The study of flags.

**YAFFLE**
Green woodpecker.

**WALLOP**
To strike hard, to defeat.

**WHIRLIGIG**
A spinning top.

**WOBBEGONG**
An Australian shark.

**ZANY**
Amusingly crazy or clownish.

# ODDITIES

*The English language abounds in oddities and eccentricities. Here are just a few to admire.*

**POLISH:** The only word in the English language that changes it's pronunciation when capitalised.
*My Polish relatives gave me some furniture but I have to polish it every week.*

**MONTH, SILVER, PURPLE, ORANGE:** There are no words in English to rhyme perfectly with these four.

**DREAMT:** The only word in English ending with an "mt"

**SUBCONTINENTAL:** The only word with all the vowels in reverse order.

**45 LETTERS :** The world's *longest-named lake* has 45 letters Lake Chargoggagoggmanchauggagoggchaubunagungamaugg.

**TWO Us TOGETHER:** Only four words in English — muumuu, residuum, vacuum, and continuum.

**Two-syllable words which become one-syllable words when you add a letter(s):** *Ague/Plague, Ague/Vague, Rugged/Shrugged, Boa/Boat, Ragged/Dragged, Naked/ Snaked, Sour/Source.*

**Ewe and You**—sound exactly the same but have no letters in common. Other examples are *Eye/I, Oh/Eau.*

**I, You, The** and **A** are the most commonly spoken English words.

**INTERCHANGEABILITY:** Contains these numbers — *Three, Eight, Nine, Ten, Thirteen, Thirty, Thirty-Nine, Eighty, Eighty-Nine, Ninety,* and *Ninety-Eight.*

**INTESTINES:** each of its letters occurs twice.

**MONDAY:** the only day of the week having an anagram —dynamo.

# 'OLOGIES

*The study of a field of knowledge is an XXX-ology.*
*Please note: only one spelling has been chosen however there*
*are alternate versions.*

*Said Freud, a big noise in psychology*
*To Durkheim whose stock-in-trade was sociology,*
*"Dis simply must stop!*
*It simply won't do!*
*Ve are drowning in 'ology stew!"*

## A

* Acarology, the study of ticks and mites
* Actinology, the study of the effect of light on chemicals
* Aetiology, the medical study of the causation of disease
* Agrobiology, the study of plant nutrition and growth in relation to soil conditions
* Andrology, the study of male health and disease
* Anaesthesiology, the study of anaesthesia and anaesthetics; a branch of medicine
* Angiology, the study of the anatomy of blood and lymph vascular systems
* Anthropology, the study of humans
* Arachnology, the study of spiders and their kin
* Archaeology, the study of ancient history through excavation
* Astrology, the study of purported influences of stars on human affairs
* Audiology, the study of hearing; a branch of medicine
* Axiology, the study of the nature of values and value judgements

## B

* Bacteriology, the study of bacteria
* Banaleology, the study of underwhelming language
* Biology, the study of life
* Biometeorology, the study of the effects of atmospheric conditions on living organisms

# C

* Campanology, the study and the art of bell ringing
* Cardiology, the study of the heart
* Carpology, the study of the structure of seeds and fruit
* Cerealogy, the study of crop circles
* Cetology, the study of marine mammals
* Chronology, the study of things in order of time
* Climatology, the study of the climate
* Conchology, the study of shells and of molluscs
* Cosmology, the study of the cosmos or our place in it.
* Craniology, the study of the characteristics of the skull
* Criminology, the scientific study of crime.
* Cryptology, the study of how to encrypt and decrypt secret messages
* Cynology, the study of dogs
* Cytology, the study of cells

# D

* Demonology, the study of demons
* Dendrochronology, the study of the age of trees and the records in their rings
* Dendrology, the study of trees
* Dermatology, the field of medicine that deals with the skin

# E

* Ecology, the study of the interrelationships between living organisms and their environment
* Ecophysiology, the study of the interrelationship between an organism's physical functioning and its environment
* Egyptology, the study of the ancient Egyptians
* Embryology, the study of embryos
* Endocrinology, the study of internal secretory glands
* Entomology, the study of insects
* Epidemiology, the study of epidemics
* Epistemology, the study of the nature and origins of knowledge
* Ethnology, the study of race
* Ethology, the study of animal behaviour
* Etymology, the study of word origins
* Evolutionary biology, the study of the process of biological evolution

* Exobiology, the study of life in outer space

## G

* Gastroenterology - diseases of stomach and intestines
* Gemmology , the study of gemstones and ornamental materials
* Genealogy, the study of relationships within families particularly with a view to constructing family trees
* Geochronology, the study of the age of the Earth
* Geology, the study of the Earth's crust
* Geomorphology, the study of present-day land forms, traditionally on Earth but with increasing frequency on nearby planetary objects
* Gerontology, the study of old age
* Glaciology, the study of glaciers
* Graphology, the study of handwriting for the purpose of analysing the character of the writer
* Gynaecology, the study of medicine relating to women

## H

* Haematology, the study of blood
* Heliology, the study of the Sun
* Helminthology, the study of parasitic worms
* Hepatology, the study of the liver; a branch of medicine
* Herbology, the study of the therapeutic use of plants
* Herpetology, the study of reptiles and amphibians
* Histology, the study of living tissues
* Histopathology, the study of the (microscopic) structure of diseased tissues
* Horology, the study of making timepieces, measuring time and timekeeping
* Hydrogeology, the study of underground water
* Hydrology, the study of water

## I

* Ichthyology, the study of fish
* Ichnology, the study of fossil footprints, tracks and burrows
* Immunology, the study of the immune system

## K

* Killology, the study of human beings killing other human beings

* Kinaesiology, the study of movement in relation to human anatomy; a branch of medicine
* Kymatology, the study of waves or wave motions

## L

* Lithology, the study of rocks
* Lymphology, the study of the lymph system and glands

## M

* Malacology, the study of molluscs
* Mammology, the study of mammals
* Meteorology, the study of weather
* Methodology, (properly) the study of methods
* Metrology, the study of measurement
* Microbiology, the study of micro organisms and their effects on humans
* Mineralogy, the study of minerals
* Morphology, the study of forms; more precisely the study of the grammatical structure of words, a branch of linguistics
* Musicology, the study of music
* Myology, the scientific study of muscles
* Myrmecology, the study of ants
* Mythology, the study of myths

## N

* Nanotechnology, the study and design of machines at the molecular level
* Neonatology, the study of diseases and the care of newborn infants; a branch of paediatrics
* Nephology, the study of clouds
* Nephrology, the study of the kidneys and their diseases, a branch of medicine
* Neurology, the study of nerves
* Neuropathology, the study of neural diseases
* Neurophysiology, the study of the functions of the nervous system
* Nosology, the study of classification of diseases
* Numerology, the study of numbers (non-mathematical)

## O

* Oceanology, the study of oceans
* Odontology, the study of the structure, development, and abnormalities of the teeth

ORTHOGRAPHY - STUDY OF CORRECT SPELLING OF WORDS

* Oncology, the study of cancer
* Oenology, the study of wine and wine making
* Ontology, the study of existence
* Oology, the study of eggs
* Ophthalmology, the study of the eyes
* Ornithology, the study of birds
* Orology, the study of mountains and their mapping
* Osteology, the study of bones
* Otology, the study of the structure, function, and pathology of the ear

## P

* Palaentology, the study of ancient creatures
* Paleoclimatology, the study of climate prior to the widespread availability of records of temperature, precipitation, and other instrumental data
* Palynology, the study of pollen
* Parapsychology, the study of paranormal or psychic phenomena that defy conventional scientific explanations
* Parasitology, the study of parasites
* Pathology, the study of illness
* Pedology, the study of soil
* Penology, the study of prison management and criminal rehabilitation.
* Petrology, the study of rocks
* Pharmacology, the study of drugs
* Phenomenology, the study and science of phenomena as distinct from the science of actual existence or being; also a movement founded by Husserl which studies conscious experience without its metaphysical concerns
* Phonology, the study of vocal sounds
* Phrenology, the derivation of a person's character traits, by studying the shape of their skull
* Physiology, the study of bodies
* Phytology, the study of plants; botany
* Pneumology, the study of the lungs and related organs; a branch of medicine

* Primatology, the study of primates
* Psychobiology, the study and psychology of organisms with regard to their functions and structures
* Psychology, the study of mental processes in humans
* Pyrology, the study of fire

## R

* Radiology, the study of rays, usually ionising radiation
* Reflexology, the study of links to the foot and the body organ systems
* Rheology, the study of flow
* Rheumatology, the study of rheumatic diseases, a branch of medicine
* Rhinology, the study of the nose and its diseases

## S

* Scatology, the study of swear words. Related to "scat singing" in Jazz music.
* Seismology, the study of earthquakes
* Selenology, the study of the moon
* Semiology the study of signs
* Serology, the study of blood serum
* Sexology, the study of sex
* Sinology, the study of China
* Sociology, the study of society
* Sociobiology, the study of the effect of evolution on ethology
* Speleology, the study or exploration of caves
* Stomatology, the study of the mouth and its diseases
* Symptomatology, the study of symptoms

## T

* Teleology, the study of ends or final causes
* Theology, the study of God
* Tocology, the study of childbirth
* Topology, the mathematical study of closeness and connectedness
* Toxicology, the study of poisons
* Tribology, the study of friction and lubrication
* Typology, the study of classification

## U

* Urology, the study and treatment of diseases of the urogenital tract, a branch of medicine

## V

* Venereology, the study of venereal diseases
* Vexillology, the study of flags
* Victimology, the study of victims of crime, often applied to characterizing the criminal
* Virology, the study of viruses
* Volcanology (also spelled vulcanology), the study of volcanoes and related phenomena

## X — Z

* Xenobiology, the study of non-terrestrial life
* Xylology, the study of wood
* Zoology, the study of animals
* Zymology, the study of fermentation

# BEFUDDLED?

*Eprigram / Epigraph / Epitaph*
An epigram is a short poem with a witty ending.
An epigraph is a short quotation or pithy statement put at the beginning of a book.
An epitaph is a phrase commemorating someone who has died, often inscribed on the tombstone.

*Euphuism / Euphemism*
Euphuism is a high blown style or speaking or writing.
Euphemism is the use of an inoffensive phrase instead of one considered offensive.

*Factious / Factitious / Fractious*
Factious means 'characterised by dissension.'
Factitious means 'contrived or artificial.'
Fractious means 'irritable or peevish.'

*Incipient / Insipid*
Incipient means 'beginning to be or appear"
Insipid means 'uninteresting or dull'

# BURBLE, BUZZ, CLANG

*There's a delightful word for describing 'Wolf' words in wolf's clothing so to speak. And the word is —*
*Onomatopoeia!*

| | |
|---|---|
| Bang | The sound of fireworks. |
| Bark | The sound vocalised by a medium-sized dog. |
| Bing | The sound of the oven timer when the cookies are done. |
| Blippity-Blop-Blop-Ver-Slotch | |
| | The sound of a stomach illness . |
| Boing | The sound of a roomful of springs. |
| Bong | The sound of church bells on a Sunday morn. |
| Boom | The sound of an imploding TV vacuum tube. |
| Burble | The sound of a lidded pot brimming with boiling water. |
| Buzz | The sound of ten thousand bees. |
| Clang | The sound of a hammer hitting a sheet of metal. |
| Click | The warning sound of small firearms. |
| Crackle | The sound of dry wood on a campfire. |
| Crash | The imminent sound of playing baseball in the house. |
| Ding | The first sound of the average doorbell. |
| Dong | The second sound of the average doorbell. |
| Fizz | The sound of a bottle of well-shaken Coke. |
| Goosh | The sound of a dam bursting open. |
| Gurgle | The last sound water makes before going down the drain. |
| Huff | The sound Chubby makes when we punch him in the stomach. |
| Hiss | The sound of nearby snakes or low tyres (neither of which is good). |
| Hum | The sound of the radiator in the library. |
| Ka-blam | The sound of an exploding grenade. |

| | |
|---|---|
| Kerplunk | The sound of a wrench being dropped into a water-filled basin. |
| Lub-dub | The sound that the heart makes according to anatomy textbooks. |
| Meow | The sound of a real cat. |
| Moo | The sound of a stereotypical cow. |
| Murmur | The sound heard around the work place on the day after a sacking or corporate scandal. |
| Ping | The sound of a crescent wrench hitting a cement floor. |
| Purr | The sound of a very happy cat or well-groomed automobile. |
| Ring | The sound of kids on bicycles riding towards the ice cream truck. |
| Szhoom | The sound of a light sabre cutting through the air. |
| Splash | The sound of the bow breaking through the waves. |
| Squeak | The incessant sound pouring out from a roommate's chair. |
| Thud | The sound of a brick falling to the earth. |
| Thwap | The sound of skin on skin. |
| Tick | The sound of the Grandfather clock when the pendulum is on the left. |
| Tock | The sound of the Grandfather clock when the pendulum is on the right. |
| Whirr | The sound of an electric can opener that has seen better days. |
| Whiz | The sound of a 60-mph baseball three inches from your head. |
| Woosh | The sound that every flying super hero makes on takeoff. |
| Wop | The sound of a wet rag thrown onto a greasy counter top. |
| Yap | The sound of a small annoying dog. |

# BUILT-IN CONTRADICTIONS

*It can happen in a phrase or it can occur in a sentence. The technical name for this is oxymoron, plural oxymora. Certain individuals excelled at this art word form — WC Fields and Samuel Goldwyn for instance.*

* A little pain never hurt anyone.

* A unified, neutral Germany? Given that nation's heritage, such a phrase may prove to be the oxymoron of the decade.
  — *Kevin M. Matarese*, Fulda, West Germany; as seen in "Letters", Time magazine, p. 5, March 5, 1990.

* A verbal contract isn't worth the paper it's written on. Include me out. — *Samuel Goldwyn*

* Cum tacent, clamant. When they are silent, they shout.
  — *Cicero*

* Gentlemen, I want you to know that I am not always right, but I am never wrong. — *Samuel Goldwyn*

* Goes (Went) over like a lead balloon.

* Honk if you are against noise pollution!

* I'll give you a definite maybe. — *Samuel Goldwyn*

* I'm not going to say, "I told you so."

* I am a deeply superficial person. — *Andy Warhol*

* I'm proud of my humility.

* I can resist everything but temptation. — *Oscar Wilde*

* If Roosevelt were alive, he'd turn over in his grave.
  — *Samuel Goldwyn*

* If I could drop dead right now, I'd be the happiest man alive! — *Samuel Goldwyn*

* If you fall and break your legs, don't come running to me.
  — *Samuel Goldwyn*

* I never put on a pair of shoes until I've worn them five years. — *Samuel Goldwyn*

* It isn't an optical illusion. It just looks like one.

* It's more than magnificent. It's mediocre.
  — *Samuel Goldwyn*

* May I ask a question?
* No one goes to that restaurant any more—it's always too crowded. (*attributed to Yogi Berra*)
* Our comedies are not to be laughed at. — *Sam Goldwyn*
* Parting is such sweet sorrow. — *William Shakespeare*
* Procrastination means never having to say you're sorry.
* Professional certification for car people may sound like an oxymoron. —*The Wall Street Journal*, page B1, Tuesday, July 17, 1990.
* Referring to a book: I read part of it all the way through. — *Samuel Goldwyn*
* Smoking is the leading cause of statistics.
* Some bachelors want a meaningful overnight relationship.
* Talking about a piece of movie dialogue: Let's have some new cliches. — *Samuel Goldwyn*
* The scene is dull. Tell him to put more life into his dying. — *Samuel Goldwyn*
* Thank God I'm an atheist.
* We're overpaying him, but he's worth it. — *Sam Goldwyn*
* His honour rooted in dishonour stood,
  And faith unfaithful kept him falsely true.
  — *Alfred Lord Tennyson*
* The good oxymoron, to define it by a self-illustration, must be a planned inadvertency. — *Wilson Follett*
* An Irishman is never at peace except when he's fighting.
* I marvel at the strength of human weakness.
* Always be sincere, even when you don't mean it.
  — *Irene Peter*
* Live within your income, even if you have to borrow to do so. — *Josh Billings*
* Of course I can keep secrets. It's the people I tell them to that can't keep them. — *Anthony Haden-Guest*
* The best cure for insomnia is to get a lot of sleep
  — *W. C. Fields*

* I distinctly remember forgetting that. — *Clara Barton*
* We must believe in free will. We have no choice.
  — *Isaac B. Singer*
* I'd give my right arm to be ambidextrous.
* I never liked you, and I always will. — *Samuel Goldwyn*
* Why don't you pair 'em up in threes? — *Yogi Berra*
* Our similarities are different. — *Dale Berra*, son of Yogi
* After Donald Trump's stretch limousine was stolen and found undamaged a few blocks away; he said, "Nothing was stolen. I had an honest thief."— *International Herald Tribune,* page 3, March 2, 1992
* Some bird populations soaring down — Headline of an article in *Science News*, page 126, February 20, 1993.
* *Triumph without Victory*, The Unreported History of the Persian Gulf War, — Headline published in the *U.S. News & World Report*, 1992.
* An empty cab drove up and Sarah Bernhardt got out.
  — *Arthur Baer*, American comic and columnist
* She used to diet on any kind of food she could lay her hands on. — *Arthur Baer*, American comic and columnist
* The first condition of immortality is death.
  — *Stanislaw Lec*
* As famous as the unknown soldier.
* I must follow the people. Am I not their leader?
  — *Benjamin Disraeli*
* Hegel was right when he said that we learn from history that man can never learn anything from history.
  — *George Bernard Shaw*
* William Safire's rules for writing as seen in *The New York Times*

  Do not put statements in the negative form.

  And don't start sentences with a conjunction.

  If you reread your work, you will find on rereading that a great deal of repetition can be avoided by rereading and editing.

Never use a long word when a diminutive one will do.

Unqualified superlatives are the worst of all.

If any word is improper at the end of a sentence, a linking verb is.

Avoid trendy locutions that sound flaky.

Never, ever use repetitive redundancies.

Also, avoid awkward or affected alliteration.

Last, but not least, avoid clichés like the plague.

* Everyone writes on the walls except me. — Said to be graffiti seen in Pompeii

* I tripped over a hole that was sticking up out of the ground.

* I don't think anyone should write their autobiography until after they're dead. — *Samuel Goldwyn*

* This page intentionally left blank.

* Evil isn't all bad.

* I disagree with unanimity.

* It's a step forward although there was no progress. *President Hosni Mubarak* of Egypt attempting to put the best face on a disappointing summit meeting between President Clinton and the Syrian President Hafez Assad.

# BEFUDDLED?

*Fervent / Fervid*
Both have a similar meaning, ardent or intense, but fervent, has positive connotations, whereas fervid has a negative nuance, e.g. a fervid devotion to freedom; a fervid interest in sex.

# OXYMORA GALORA!

*Everyday self-contradictory terms.*

accidentally on purpose
active retirement
ageing yuppie
agree to disagree
a little pregnant
bad luck
balanced insanity
balding hair
benevolent despot
benign neglect
birthday suit
cheerfully cynical
civil disobedience
civilised warfare
clearly ambiguous
clearly confused
constant change
constructive ambiguity
controlled enthusiasm
corporate planning
correctional institution
criminal justice
customer satisfaction
definite maybe
eloquent silence
ergonomic keyboard
eschew obfuscation
explicit innuendo

expressive silence
extremely average
extremely bland
extremely neutral
fail safe
football scholarship
fresh dried fruit
friendly argument
friendly fire
fuzzy logic
genuine fake
happy apathy
hasten slowly
hopelessly optimistic
idiot savant
junk food
just war
justifiable genocide
known-covert operation
kosher ham
larger half
less is more
living end
living fossil
military peace
more unique
most unique
negative growth

new cliche

noble savage

non-stick glue

oddly appropriate

old news

one size fits all

open secret

organised chaos

painless torture

passive confrontation

passively aggressive

pious atheist

planned serendipity

psychiatric care

public secret

quiet tirade

random order

regular special

safe and sane fireworks

safe guns

safe sex

same difference

school vacation

second best

semiprecious

semiprivate

serious humour

sight unseen

simple computers

single thought

small fortune

smaller half

socialist worker

somewhat functional

somewhat legal

speed limit

spendthrift

stealth bomber

straight angle

subjective data

synthetic-natural gas

tax cut

tense calm

tentative conclusion

terribly enjoyable

tomorrow today

totalitarian democracy

traditionally radical

truth in advertising

turned up missing

unbiased opinion

unbiased journalism

uncommonly common

unknown identity

unrepeatable pleonasm

unwelcome recess

user friendly

vaguely aware

virtual reality

waiting patiently

war games

waste management

white rose

# BODY PARTS MYSTERY

Where can a man buy a cap for his knee,
Or the key to a lock of his hair?
Can his eyes be called an academy
Because there are pupils there?

Is the crown of your head where jewels are found?
Who travels the bridge of your nose?
If you wanted to shingle the roof of your mouth,
Would you use the nails on your toes?

Can you sit in the shade of the palm of your hand,
Or beat on the drum of your ear?
Can the calf in your leg eat the corn off your toe?
Then why not grown corn on the ear?

Can the crook in your elbow be sent to jail?
If so, just what did he do?
How can you sharpen your shoulder blades?
I'll be darned if I know, do you?

— *author unknown*

# THE GIFT OF LANGUAGE

Language is a city to the building of which every human being
brought a stone.
— *Ralph Waldo Emerson*

We die.
That may be the meaning of life.
But we do language.
That may be the measure of our lives.
— *Toni Morrison*

We live at the level of our language.
Whatever we can articulate
we can imagine or explore.
All you have to do to educate a child is leave
them alone and teach them to read.
The rest is brainwashing.
— *Ellen Gilcrist*

---

*I am* is reportedly the shortest sentence in the English
language. Could it be that *I do* is the longest sentence?

If lawyers are disbarred and clergymen defrocked, doesn't
it follow that electricians can be delighted, musicians
denoted, cowboys deranged, models deposed, tree surgeons
debarked, and dry cleaners depressed?

Do Roman paramedics refer to IV's as *4's*?

By rearranging a ten-word sentence in the English
language into every conceivable combination, whether
grammatical or not – there are 3,628,800 possible
combinations.

---

# FRESHLY COINED

*Fast food, the Information Superhighway, 24/7 customer service, active ageing, quality time, while-u-wait.*

*These newly minted words are intended to give a kaleidoscopic impression of the bizarre all-you-can-eat-see-read-do-believe culture we inhabit!*

## AUDIOPHILE
Lover of audio equipment and media, an avid collector of same.

## BAGGRAVATION
Annoyance and anger felt at airport when one's bags have not turned up at the baggage carousel even though everyone else's bags have.

## BEEPER MEDICINE
Reactive medical practice that responds chiefly to pages and other emergency call outs.

## CARCOONING
Using your car for working, playing, eating, dressing, grooming and other things normally performed either at home or at work.

## DASHBOARD DINING
To reflect the increasing trend for commuters to eat meals while driving.

## DISORIENT EXPRESS
A state of confusion

## DOOR DWELL
The amount of time it takes for an elevator door to close after boarding it.  Does it sometimes seem like infinity?

## CHURNOVER
Excessive buying and selling of shares by a stockbroker.

## COMPETITIVE COMPASSION
Contributing to a charity in a greater amount than others  for recognition.

## EARWITNESS
A individual who hears an event occur, especially when they are prepared to give testimony to the fact.

## FOOD COURT MULTI CULTURALISM
A belief that you are gaining an appreciation of other cultures through the practice of eating other ethnic cuisine in mall food courts.

## FREEMIUM
A business model offering basic services free, but charging a premium for special features.

## FURTHER FETCHED
Beyond far-fetched.

## GLOBOBOSS
A cosmopolitan executive who operates business comfortably without borders.

## HACTIVIST
An computer hacker who furthers an activist agenda by hacking into computer systems.

## INFORMATION FATIGUE SYNDROME
The overwhelming stress of having to deal with an overload of information.

## JAPANIMATION
The kind of animation originating in Japan having futuristic and robotic themes.

## M<sup>C</sup> JOB
A lowly paid service related job with little prestige and very little chance of advancement.

## MEANDERTHAL
Someone shambling along aimlessly in front of someone else who's in a bit of a hurry.

## MICROVACATION
A very short vacation – maybe just a half-day!

## MUCUS TROOPER
A stoic who insists on coming in to work even though they are sneezing and coughing all over the place.

## NETIZEN
Someone spending an inordinate amount of time on the Net.

## POPAGANDA
Music popular with the general public but also promoting a particular ethos or idea.

## POOPER-SCOOPER
A device on the end of a long pole used for picking up doggie-do.

## PUPPERWARE
Dog toys and accessories, especially ones demonstrated at home parties.

## RAPTIVIST
A rapper who is an activist.

## RETAIL THERAPY
A tendency to purchase gifts and goods for oneself to feel happier and more fulfilled.

## RINGXIETY
Confusion caused by cell phone ringing in a group of people and no-one quite sure if it's their phone.

## SARCASTROPHE
When humorous sarcasm fails abysmally and turns into more of a tragedy.

## SHOPAHOLIC
Someone addicted to shopping.

## SNAIL MAIL
The standard form of mail delivery when letters, documents and parcels are physically transported from one location to another.

## SLACKIVIST
An activist seeking causes and projects that require the least amount of effort.

## STALKERAZZI
Tabloid journalists who unscrupulously and sedulously pursue celebrities, shadowing their every move.

## STRESS PUPPY
Someone continually moaning about the stress in their life, but not prepared to do anything about it.

## SUDDEN WEALTH SYNDROME
The anxiety and stress brought about by a sudden accumulation of unaccustomed riches.

## SWOOSHTIKA
A derogatory reference to the Nike tick.

## VELOCITISE
To cause a person to become used to a fast speed.

## TELEVANGELIST
An evangelist who frequently uses the TV to prosletyse his/her religious message.

## WELLDERLY
Healthy, wealthy and optionally wise.

## WHOOPIE
Well-off older person.

## WORDROBE
A person's vocabulary.

Ours is the age of substitutes:
Instead of language we have jargon;
instead of principles, slogans;
and instead of genuine ideas,
bright suggestions.
— *Eric Bentley*

# WOLVES IN CUBS' CLOTHING

*There are perennial words and terms that appear to be in vogue. Some have in fact been doing the rounds since the sixties — here are some that might surprise you.*

Affirmative action (1968)

Alternative medicine (1967)

Backhander (1960)

Biodegradable (1963)

Breathalyser (1960)

Byte (1964)

Cable television (1966)

Chequebook journalism (1963)

Computer dating (1968)

Convenience store (1965)

Credibility gap (1968)

Flexible response (1967)

Fuzzy logic ( 1965)

Gas guzzler (1968)

Global village (1967)

Glue sniffing (1963)

Greenhouse effect (1962)

Hard copy (1964)

Infotainment (1960)

Intensive Care (1963)

Junk mail (1967)

Lateral thinking (1966)

Learning curve (1967)

# THIS-ISM, THAT-ISM

*Since the early 1970s -ISMs have sprouted forth in an ever-accelerating attempt to cover discriminations against every nuance of the human condition. Take a look at these:*

| ISM | Discrimination against | Year |
|---|---|---|
| Ableism | The disabled | 1981 |
| Adultism | Children | 1985 |
| Alphabetism | Name's initial letter appearing later in the alphabet | 1988 |
| Beardism | Bearded men | 1991 |
| Bodyism | Body size or shape | 1991 |
| Bookism | Non-book readers | 1979 |
| Breastism | Breast size | 1991 |
| Faceism | Ugly, or not good-looking people | 1992 |
| Faithism | Religion | 1994 |
| Feelism | Animals who are slimy, scaly, crawly or smelly | 1992 |
| Foodism | Plain or unhealthy food eaters | 1985 |
| Heightism | Height (esp. small people) | 1980 |
| Sightism | Blindness or visual impairment | 1991 |
| Smellism | Smell | 1991 |
| Wineism | People who drink inferior wines | 1991 |
| Voiceism | Voice | 1992 |

I used to think I was poor.
Then they told me I wasn't poor, I was needy.
Then they told me it was self-defeating to think of myself as needy.
I was deprived.
(Oh not deprived but rather underprivileged)
Then they told me that underprivileged was overused.
I was disadvantaged.
I still don't have a dime.
But I have a great vocabulary.
—*Jules Pfeiffer*

# FORWARDS, BACKWARDS

*Read it forwards, read it backwards, it's the same!*

*'Tis what we call a palindrome!*

Don't nod
Dogma: I am God
Never odd or even
Too bad — I hid a boot
Rats live on no evil star
No trace; not one carton
Was it Eliot's toilet I saw?
Murder for a jar of red rum
May a moody baby doom a yam?
Go hang a salami; I'm a lasagna hog!
Satan, oscillate my metallic sonatas!
A Toyota! Race fast     safe car: a Toyota
Straw? No, too stupid a fad; I put soot on warts
Are we not drawn onward, we few, drawn onward to new era?
Doc Note: I dissent. A fast never prevents a fatness. I diet on cod
No, it never propagates if I set a gap or prevention
Anne, I vote more cars race Rome to Vienna
Sums are not set as a test on Erasmus
Kay, a red nude, peeped under a yak
Some men interpret nine memos
Campus Motto: Bottoms up, Mac
Go deliver a dare, vile dog!
Madam, in Eden I'm Adam
Oozy rat in a sanitary zoo
Ah, Satan sees Natasha
Lisa Bonet ate no basil
Do geese see God?
God saw I was dog
Dennis sinned

# RIDDLES

What word becomes a palindrome when viewed upside down
and backwards?
### SWIMS

Pronounced as one letter but written with three,
only two different letters are used to make me.
I'm double, I'm single I'm black, blue, and gray.
I'm read from both ends and the same either way.
### EYE

What word, when written in capital letters,
is the same forwards, backwards and upside down?
### NOON

What call for help, when written in capital or lower case,
is the same forwards, backwards and upside down?
### SOS

# MORE PALINDROMES

A poem, a carol, or a cameo, Pa?

Ana, nab a banana.

Anne, I vote more cars race Rome to Vienna.

Boston did not sob.

Cain: A maniac!

Dammit, I'm mad!

Delia sailed, Eva waved, Elias ailed.

Delia saw I was ailed.

Denim axes examined.

Desserts I desire not, so long no lost one rise distressed.

Devil never even lived.

Dew on roses or no, wed.

Did Hannah say as Hannah did?

Do geese see God?

Dr. Awkward

Drab as a fool, aloof as a bard.

Erin is in ire.

Evil olive.

Face decaf?

Flee to me, remote elf.

Gnu hung.

Go deliver a dare, vile dog.

Golf? No sir, prefer prison-flog.

He lived as a devil, eh?

Hot tuba. Put it up a butt, oh.

I did, did I?

I saw I was I.

I was sad — no Hondas saw I.

I won, Karen, an era know I.

Knits stink!

Late fetal.

Lay a wallaby baby ball away, Al.

Lepers repel.

Live not on evil, madam, live not on evil.

Live on evasions? No, I save no evil.

Ma is a nun, as I am.

Ma is as selfless as I am.

Man, Oprah's sharp on AM.

Mix a maxim.

Mom's Dad & Dad's Mom!

No evil I did, I live on.

No garden, one dragon.

No, it is opposition.

No — noose be soon on!

No, Sir, panic is a basic in a prison.

Noon.

Now Eve, we're here — we've won.

Now I see, referees, I won.

Now, Sir, a war is won!

Now's evil for evil? Ah, a liver of lives won!

Panic in a Titanic? I nap.

Parkay Yak Rap.

Potato idiot atop.

Puff in, sniff up!

Pull a bat, I hit a ball up.

Pull up if I pull up.

Put a crow, a camel, a mini male macaw, or cat up.

"Q": a F.A.Q.

Radar.

Rae! Bite yon no yeti bear!

Red rum, sir, is murder.

Reviled did I live, said I, as evil I did deliver.

Rise, take lame female Kate, sir.

Rob a loneliness? Senile, no labor.

Seen knees.

Six ate nine taxis.

Slap a ham on Omaha, pals.

Slap my gym pals.

Sleep on no peels.

Smart ewes use wet rams.

So many dynamos.

So, G. Rivera's tots are virgos.

So, Ida, adios!

So, Mama, I won — now I am Amos!

Solo gigolos.

Solos.

Stack cats.

Star comedy by Democrats.

Straw warts.

Stunts is. Niece insist nuts.

Tango gnat.

Tarzan raised a Desi Arnaz rat.

Ten animals I slam in a net.

Tennis: Tip spits in net.

Title fit — I felt it!

To Idi Amin: I'm a idiot!

Top spot.

Top step's pup's pet spot.

Tuna nut.

Ungate me, Vic, I've met a gnu.

Vegetable was I ere I saw Elba, Tegev.

War, sir, is raw.

Warsaw was raw.

Was it a car or a cat I saw?

We few.

Wonder if Sununu's fired now?

Wonton? Not now.

Xerox a mama, Max, O Rex.

Yo, oy.

Yoba saw I was a boy.

You bat one in, resign in evening. Is Ernie not a buoy?

Zeus was deified, saw Suez.

---

When the silences are no longer awkward,
you know you are around friends.
— *Unknown*

You have not converted a man
because you have silenced him.
— *John Morley (Rousseau)*

# INSIGHTS INTO WRITING

Every man usually has something he can do better
than anyone else. Usually it is reading his own
handwriting.
— *Author unknown*

My aim is to put down on paper
what I see and what
I feel in the best and simplest way.
— *Ernest Hemingway*

Writers would be warm, loyal,  and otherwise
terrific people — if only they'd stop writing.
— *Laura Miller*

Fame often makes a writer vain,
but seldom makes him proud.
— *W. H Auden*

Writing is like cooking ... if you spill something,
you should make it look like part of the act.
— *John Keeble*

Writing is a lot like sex.
At first you do it
because you like it.
Then you find yourself doing
it for a few close friends and people you like.
But if you're any good at all ... you end up doing
it for money.
— *Author unknown*

# THE QUICK BROWN FOX

*The one we know the best is "The quick brown fox jumped over
the lazy dog". Can you remember it from school days, and
when you first learnt the keyboard? A sentence using every
letter of the alphabet at least once is called a pangram.*

A large fawn jumped quickly over white zinc boxes.

A poor Zimbabwe vet, fearing ghosts, quickly joined an
exodus.

A quart jar of oil mixed with zinc oxide makes a very bright
paint.

A quick brown fox jumps over the lazy dog.

As we explored the gulf of Zanzibar, we quickly moved closer
to the jutting rocks.

By Jove, my quick study of lexicography won a prize.

Cozy sphinx waves quart jug of bad milk.

Crazy Fredrick bought many very exquisite opal jewels.

Ebenezer unexpectedly bagged two tranquil aardvarks with
his jiffy vacuum cleaner.

Exquisite farm wench gives body jolt to prize stinker.

Fabled reader with jaded, roving eye seized by quickened
impulse to expand budget.

Five big quacking zephyrs jolt my wax bed.

Five jumbo oxen graze quietly with packs of dogs.

Five or six big jet planes zoomed quickly by the tower.

Five wine experts jokingly quizzed chablis sample.

Freight to me sixty dozen quart jars and twelve black pans.

Glum, wavy-haired ex-con bequeaths fake topaz jewel.

Good, blind Jake vowed to frequent Zoi and Max's eunuch party!

Grumpy wizards make toxic brew for the evil Queen and Jack.

I was temporarily forced to zig-zag and quiver furiously around big junky xylophones.

Jack in the Box quickly varied its menu with fudge and pizza.

Jackdaws love my big sphinx of quartz.

Jacqueline was vexed by the folks who go the money prizes.

Jump by vow of quick, lazy strength in Oxford.

Jumpy wizard quit having black foxes.

Jumpy zebra vows to quit thinking coldly of sex.

King Alexander was just partly overcome after quizzing Diogenes in his tub.

Lazy movers quit hard packing of jewelry boxes.

My grandfather picks up quartz and valuable onyx jewels.

My help squeezed back in again after six and joined the weavers.

Pangrams have subjects like "dewy fox quiz."

Perhaps President Clinton's amazing sax skills will be judged quite favorably.

Prized waxy jonquils choke big farm vats.

Questions of a zealous nature have become by degrees petty.

The public was amazed to view the quickness and dexterity of the juggler.

The risque gown marked a very brazen exposure of juicy flesh.

The sex life of the woodchuck is a provocative question for most vertebrate zoology majors.

Two joyful vixens squirt milk upon the caged zebra.

Up at the zoo a roving ox was quickly fed bug jam.

You go tell that vapid existentialist quack Freddy Nietzsche that he can just bite me, twice.

# TURNS OF PHRASE

*Idiom is an accepted phrase or expression with a meaning different than the literal interpretation of the words. It is interesting to explore the origins of phrases. Here's a taster.*

## Agony column
*A newspaper or magazine column where the readers ask their tormented questions about love and loss and the meaning of life, while the agony aunt or uncle deigns to give advice.*

The agony column used to be the one where postings were made for missing relatives or friends.

## Armed to the teeth
*To be heavily armed*
Pirate parlance in Port Royal Jamaica in the 1600's. Having only single-shot black-powder weapons and cutlasses, they would carry many of these weapons at once to keep up the fight with whomever they wanted to divest of their riches.

## At the eleventh hour
*To raise a problem or issue right before a critical deadline*
On a 12-hour clock (rather than the 24-hour clock used by scientists, the military, et al) the hours of 12 noon and 12 midnight seem to hold special significance. Marking the transition from morning to afternoon and the end of the day, they are often used as deadlines (high noon, the stroke of midnight)

## Blow off some steam
*To relax and allow the tension to lessen.*
When steam is used to drive machinery, sometimes the steam has to be "blown off" to ease pressure in the boilers.

## Break a leg
*A wish of good luck, do well.*
Considered very bad luck in the theatre to wish anyone good luck in a direct way. So "break a leg!" is the accepted backhander for well-wishing.

## Can't hold a candle to
*Not to be nearly as skilful or competent as another.*
The flashlight of yore was the candle. When a person was
working in the dark, they needed someone to throw light on
what there were busy doing. If you say someone can't even
hold the candle, then they are hardly able to perform the task
at hand.

## Cold turkey
*To give up something abruptly without any substitutes.*
Withdrawal from tobacco or narcotics induces a pallor  and
goose bumps to the skin — a look that resembles a plucked,
cold turkey,

## Crocodile tears
*Phony tears.*
Crocodiles are thought to cry tears, not out of sentiment or
emotion, but because it aids in their digestion.

## Cut from the same cloth
*To appear or behave in the same way.*
If you're making a suit, the jacket and trousers should be cut
from the same piece of cloth to ensure a perfect match.

## Don't look a gift horse in the mouth
*Don't look for fault in a gift*
To "look a horse in the mouth" is to examine the horse's
mouth closely to determine its age (and therefore its
usefulness and/or worth)

## High on the hog
*Live or do something extravagantly.*
The best meat is on the upper portion of the pig. The well-
heeled pork lovers have always been afforded this luxury
while the underlings, downstairs staff, lesser mortals — ate
the entrails, trotters, chitterlings and so on.

## Horse of a different colour
*Unlike the subject at hand.*
Horses are registered at birth and the registration
includes a record of their colour. When a horse is sold, the
registration is also transferred. Sometimes the colour recorded
on the registration may not match the actual colour of the
horse, leading one to suspect the horse is not the one in the
registration.

## Jump on the bandwagon
*Do what everybody else is doing, follow the mob.*
Old-time political campaigns would attempt to gain
supporters with what amounted to a small parade including
a band for a candidate with sufficient support. Jumping on
the bandwagon was akin to signifying your support for this
popular candidate.

## Let the cat out of the bag
*To divulge a secret.*
At medieval markets, unscrupulous traders would display
a pig for sale. However, the pig was always given to the
customer in a bag, with strict instructions not to open the
bag until they were some distance away. The trader would
hand the customer a bag containing something that wriggled,
and it was only later that the buyer found he'd been conned
when he opened the bag revealing not a piglet, but a cat.

## Living hand to mouth
*To be so poor that there is nothing to lay away.*
During the Great Depression and other times of economic
scarcity, people often did not know when or where the next
meal was coming from.

## Long in the tooth
*To be getting old.*
The age of a horse can be roughly determined by examining
its teeth, since a horse's gums recede as they age. The longer
the teeth of a horse appear to be, the older the horse. This is
also true of humans.

## Pot to piss in
*To have some status*
In medieval London, people did not have indoor plumbing. It was common to use a chamber pot as an indoor toilet. The chamber pot could then be dumped out a window into the street gutter below. A person who did not have a "pot to piss in" was poor indeed.

## Reading the Riot Act
*To warn or threaten with punishment.*
"Reading the Riot Act" used to be a literal event. Bobbies in Britain used to read a prescribed proclamation, known as the Riot Act, before they could break up or arrest a crowd. The Miranda Rights in America would be the equivalent.

## Rule of thumb
*An estimate or some general guideline,*
Based on the use of one's thumb as a rough measurement tool. Generally correct for course measures. Most old English measures of distance were based on the body measurements of the king—the length of the foot, inch (thumb tip to first knuckle), cubit (elbow-to-fingertip), and yard (nose-to-fingertip)

## Thumbs up
*To give approval.*
It is attributed to the ancient Romans and the Gladiators who fought in the Coliseum. If Caesar judged the loser had fought bravely enough, his life would be spared, otherwise he would be killed. The spectators signalled their vote with a "thumbs up" for life and thumbs down for death.

## Write like an angel
*To write very well.*
From Angelo Vergece, a famous 16th century calligrapher in the court of Francis 1 of France.

# REPETITIOUS REDUNDANCIES

*Oxymora have an antonym or opposite — they are pleonasms. Instead of a contradiction, there's a repetition of the first term. Here are some pleonastic quotes.*

It's déja vu all over again. — attributed to Yogi Berra

Smoking can kill you, and if you've been killed, you've lost a very important part of your life. — attributed to *Brooke Shields*

Lead-lined coffins called a health risk.

Census says rich have most of the money. (news item)

Clichés are a dime a dozen — avoid them like the plague.

Cure suggestibility with hypnosis.

I've told you a million times, "Don't exaggerate!"

Is that a mirage or am I seeing things?

It's bad luck to be superstitious.

Sometimes you can observe a lot just by watching.
— *Yogi Berra*

Half the lies our opponents tell about us are not true.

Football is an incredible game. Sometimes it's so incredible, it's unbelievable. — *Tom Landry*

When large numbers of men are unable to find work, unemployment results. — *Calvin Coolidge*

Anyone who goes to a psychiatrist ought to have his head examined. — *Samuel Goldwyn*

I never make predictions, especially about the future.
— *Samuel Goldwyn*

"In the city today, the temperature rose to 105 degrees. This sudden rise of temperature was responsible for the intolerable heat."

Trapped, like a trap in a trap. — *Dorothy Parker*

I used to be indecisive, now I'm not so sure.

He lived his life to the end.

Some people are superficial but that's just on the surface.

The world is apathetic but I don't care.

Treachery will often bring loyalty into question.

Perspective is in the eye of the beholder.

If we do not succeed, we run the risk of failure. — attributed to former US Vice-President *Dan Quayle*

# LIST OF COMMON PLEONASMS

absolutely essential
absolutely necessary
advance forward
affirmative yes
affluent rich
aid and abet
A.M. in the morning
and etc.
anonymous stranger
ATM machine
bad evil
BASIC code
basic fundamentals
blood hemorrhage
CAD design
cash money
cease and desist
close proximity
close scrutiny
cold ice
collaborate together
completely annihilated
completely blind
completely deaf
completely destroyed
completely empty
completely expired
DC current
dead corpse

definite decision
descend down
DMZ zone
doctorate degree
DOS operating system
downward descent
each and every
each per capita
eliminate altogether
end result
entirely eliminating
essential necessity
exact replica
exact same
exactly the same
extra added features
forced compulsion
foreign imports
free gift
free gratis
freezing cold
full satisfaction
frozen ice
general consensus of opinion
give and bequeath
GMT time
good benefit
growing greater

half a dozen of one and six of
   another
handwritten manuscript
have and hold
hear with one's own ears
HIV virus
hot fire
hot water heater
individual person
inquisitive busybody
intentional planning
invited guests
join together
joint collaboration
joint cooperation
killed dead
knowledgeable experts
last will and testament
live witness
long litany
major breakthrough
malignant cancer
manually by hand
many frequent
marital spouse
may possibly
mental thought
merge together
mesa table
more easier
NATO organisation
necessary essentials
negative misfortune
negative no
never, ever
new neophyte
new recruit
nocturnal-night vampires

nomenclature terms
non-reading illiterates
normal, everyday
null and void
old adage
old customs
old senior citizens
only unique
    (person, place, or thing)
past experience
past history
PC Computer
perfectly legitimate
persistent obsession
personal friend
personal friendship
personal individual
PIN number
pizza pie
play actor
please RSVP
P.M. in the evening
poisonous venoms
positive yes
postponed until later
pre planning
present incumbent
previously listed above
pruned out
quite unique
rags and tatters
real actual
redundancies, tautologies,
    and pleonasms
redundant redundancies
redundant repetitions
regular routine
repeat again

repetitious redundancies

resulting effects

retreating back

return back

revert back

rice paddy

round circle

round wheels

ruling junta

see with one's own eyes

seedling plant

sharp point

shape and form

sink down

small speck

staged scenario

successful achievement

sudden impulse

suffered poorly

sum total

technical jargon

totally demolished

totally empty

totally full

totally unnecessary

true facts

tuna fish

undergraduate student

unexpected surprise

unhealthy sickness

unmarried bachelor

unmarried old maid

wall mural

watching and observing

water hydrant

wet water

widow woman

youthful teenagers

---

The word 'set' has more definitions than any other word in the English language.

"Evian" spelled backwards is naive.

The word denim comes from 'de Nimes', or from Nimes, in France.

"Mayday" the term used for signaling help comes from "M'aidez" French for "help me"

# ROOTS AND ADD-ONS

*Are you a word detective? Words have beginnings (prefixes),*
*middles (roots) and ends (suffixes)*

*For example: mono + gam + ous*
*A beginning, a middle and an end?*

| Prefix | Meaning |
|---|---|
| act | to act |
| acu, acr, ac | needle |
| alt | high |
| anima, anim | life, mind |
| ann, enn | year |
| anthrop | man |
| aqua | water |
| arch, archi | govern, rule |
| arm | army, weapon |
| arbitr, arbiter | to judge, consider |
| art | craft, skill |
| arthr, art | segment, joint |
| aud | to hear |
| bell | war |
| biblio, bibl | book |
| bio | life |
| capit, cipit | head |
| caus | cause, case, lawsuit |
| cede | to go, yield |
| cele | honour |
| cell | to rise, project |
| cent | one hundred |
| cept, capt, cip, cap, | |
| ceive, ceipt | to take, hold, grasp |
| cert | sure, to trust |
| cess, ced | to move, withdraw |
| cid, cis | to cut off, be brief, to kill |
| circ, circum | around |
| civ | citizen |

| | |
|---|---|
| claud | close, shut, block |
| clin | to lean, lie, bend |
| cog | to know |
| column | a column |
| comput | to compute |
| cont | to join, unite |
| cor, cord, cour, card | heart |
| corp | body |
| cosm | world, order, universe |
| crac, crat | rule, govern |
| cred | believe, trust |
| crit, cris | separate, discern, judge |
| culp | fault, blame |
| curs, curr, corr | to run |
| custom | one's own |
| dem | people |
| dent, odon | tooth |
| derm | skin |
| dic, dict | to say, to speak, assert |
| duct, duc | to lead, draw |
| dur | to harden, hold out |
| ego | I |
| ethn | nation |
| equ | equal, fair |
| fac, fic, fect, fact | to make, to do |
| famil | family |
| fen | to strike |
| fer | to carry, bear, bring |
| fid | trust, faith |
| fin | to end |
| flu | to flow |
| form | shape, form |
| fort | chance, luck, strong |
| frig | cool |
| fum | smoke, scent |
| gam | marriage |
| gen | race, family, kind |
| geo | earth |

| | |
|---|---|
| gno, kno | to know |
| grad, gred, gress | step, degree, rank |
| graph, gram | write, draw, describe, record |
| grat | pleasure, thankful, goodwill, joy |
| grav, griev, grief | heavy |
| gymno | naked |
| hab | to have, hold, dwell |
| homo | man, human |
| hosp | guest, host |
| host | enemy, stranger |
| hydro | water |
| hygiene | the art of health |
| hypno | sleep |
| init | to begin, enter upon |
| jur, jus, jud | law, right |
| juven | young |
| labor, lab | work |
| lat | lateral, side, wide |
| laud | praise |
| leg, lig | law, to chose, perceive, understand |
| lev | to make light, raise, lift |
| liber, liver | free |
| lingu, langu | tongue |
| lith | stone |
| loc | place |
| locu, loqu | word, speak |
| log | idea, word, speech, reason, study |
| luc, lum | light |
| man | hand |
| mar | sea |
| med, medi | middle |
| medic | physician, to heal |
| memor | mindful |
| men, min, mon | to think, remind, advise, warn |
| ment | mind |
| meter, metr | measure |
| migr | to move, travel |
| mim | copy, imitate |

| | |
|---|---|
| mit, mis | to send |
| mono | one, on its own |
| mor | fool, manner, custom |
| morph | form |
| mort | death |
| mov, mob, mot | to move |
| mus | little mouse |
| mut | change, exchange |
| necess | unavoidable |
| neur, nerv | nerve |
| noc, nox | night, harm |
| nomen, nomin | name |
| null, nihil, nil | nothing, void |
| nym, onym, onom | name |
| opt | eye |
| ord, ordin | order |
| ortho | straight |
| par, pair | arrange, prepare, get ready, set |
| part, pars | portion, part |
| ped, pes | foot |
| pend, pond, pens | to weigh, pay, consider |
| phe, fa, fe | speak, spoken about |
| phil | love |
| phon | sound, voice |
| photo | light |
| pler | to fill |
| plic | to fold |
| plur, plus | more |
| pneu | breath |
| polis, polit | citizen, city, state |
| port | to carry |
| pos | to place, put |
| pot | powerful |
| prim, prin | first |
| priv | separate |
| prob | to prove, test |
| psych | mind, soul, spirit |
| pyr | fire |

| | |
|---|---|
| reg, rig, rect, reign | government, rule, right, straight |
| respond | to answer |
| rupt | break, burst |
| sacr, secr, sacer | sacred |
| sat | to please |
| sci | to know |
| scope | to see |
| scrib, script | to write |
| sed, sid, sess | to sit, to settle |
| sent, sens | to feel |
| sequ, secut | to follow, sequence |
| simil, simul, sembl | together, likeness, pretence |
| sol, soli | alone, lonely |
| solus | to comfort, to console |
| somn | sleep |
| son | sound |
| soph | wise |
| spec, spect, spic | to look at, behold |
| spond, spons | to pledge, promise |
| tac, tic | silent |
| techn | art, skill |
| temp | time |
| ten, tain, tent | to hold |
| tend, tens | to give heed, stretch toward |
| term | boundary, limit |
| test | to witness, affirm |
| the, them, thet | to place, put |
| theatr | to see, view |
| theo | god |
| topo | place |
| tract | to pull, draw |
| trib | to allot, give |
| vac | empty |
| ven | to come |
| ver | truth |
| vers, vert | to turn |
| vest | to adorn |
| vestig | to track |
| via | way, road |

| Suffix | Meaning |
| --- | --- |
| age | belongs to |
| ance | state of being |
| ant | thing or one who |
| ar | relating to, like |
| ary | relating to, like |
| ence | state, fact, quality |
| ent | to form |
| ic | like, having the nature |
| ine | nature of-feminine ending |
| ion, tion, ation | being, the result of |
| ism | act, condition |
| ist | one who |
| ive | of, belonging to, quality of |
| ment | a means, product, act, state |
| or | person or thing that |
| ory | place for |
| ty | condition of, quality of |

## ADJECTIVE-FORMING SUFFIXES

| Suffix | Meaning |
| --- | --- |
| able | capable of being |
| al | like, suitable for |
| ance | state of being |
| ant | thing or one who |
| ar | relating to, like |
| ary | relating to, like |
| ate | to become associated with |
| ent | to form |
| ial | function of |
| ible | capable of being |
| ic | like, having the nature of |
| ine | nature of-feminine ending |
| ive | of, belonging to, quality of |
| ory | place for |
| ous | characterized by, having quality of |

## VERB-FORMING SUFFIXES

| Suffix | Meaning |
|--------|---------|
| ate | to become associated with |
| fy | make, do |
| ise, ize | to become like |

## ADVERB-FORMING SUFFIXES

| Suffix | Meaning |
|--------|---------|
| ic | like, having the nature of |
| ly | like, to extent of |

It might take a bullett or tu
When reformers have nothing to du
They might take a shot at the Gnu,
To nock off the G,
Would fill them with glee
And wouldn't embarass the Nu.

A wise old owl lived in an oak;
The more he saw, the less he spoak.
The less he spoak,
The more he heard;
Why can't we be like that old beard?

— *author unknown*

# PRONUNCIATION

*The following verse was devised to help people learning
English as a second language, to understand the variations in
pronunciation. A Frenchman declared after reciting only six
lines, that he'd rather do six month's hard labour!*

Dearest creature in creation,
Studying English pronunciation.
I will teach you in my verse
Sounds like corpse, corps, horse, and worse.
It will keep you, Susy, busy,
Make your head with heat grow dizzy.
Tear in eye, your dress will tear.
So shall I! Oh hear my prayer.
Pray console your loving poet,
Make my coat look new, dear, sew it.


Just compare heart, beard, and heard,
Dies and diet, lord and word,
Sword and sward, retain and Britain.
(Mind the latter, how it's written.)
Made has not the sound of bade,
Say — said, pay — paid, laid, but plaid.
Now I surely will not plague you
With such words as plaque and ague.
But be careful how you speak:
Say break and steak, but bleak and streak;
Cloven, oven, how and low,
Script, receipt, show, poem, and toe.


Hear me say, devoid of trickery,
Daughter, laughter, and Terpsichore,
Typhoid, measles, topsails, aisles,
Exiles, similes, and reviles;
Scholar, vicar, and cigar,
Solar, mica, war and far;

179

One, anemone, Balmoral,
Kitchen, lichen, laundry, laurel;
Gertrude, German, wind and mind,
Scene, Melpomene, mankind.

Billet does not rhyme with ballet,
Bouquet, wallet, mallet, chalet.
Blood and flood are not like food,
Nor is mould like should and would.
Viscous, viscount, load and broad,
Toward, to forward, to reward.
And your pronunciation's OK
When you correctly say croquet,
Rounded, wounded, grieve and sleeve,
Friend and fiend, alive and live.

Ivy, privy, famous, clamour
And enamour rhyme with hammer.
River, rival, tomb, bomb, comb,
Doll and roll and some and home.
Stranger does not rhyme with anger,
Neither does devour with clangour.
Souls but foul, haunt but aunt,
Font, front, wont, want, grand, and grant,
Shoes, goes, does. Now first say finger,
And then singer, ginger, linger,
Real, zeal, mauve, gauze, gouge and gauge,
Marriage, foliage, mirage, and age.

Query does not rhyme with very,
Nor does fury sound like bury.
Dost, lost, post and doth, cloth, loth.
Job, nob, bosom, transom, oath.
Though the differences seem little,
We say actual but victual.
Refer does not rhyme with deafer.

Foeffer does, and zephyr, heifer.
Mint, pint, senate and sedate;
Dull, bull, and George ate late.
Scenic, Arabic, Pacific,
Science, conscience, scientific.

Liberty, library, heave and heaven,
Rachel, ache, moustache, eleven.
We say hallowed, but allowed,
People, leopard, towed, but vowed.
Mark the differences, moreover,
Between mover, cover;
Leeches, breeches, wise, precise,
Chalice, but police and lice;
Camel, constable, unstable,
Principle, disciple, label.

Petal, panel, and canal,
Wait, surprise, plait, promise, pal.
Worm and storm, chaise, chaos, chair,
Senator, spectator, mayor.
Tour, but our and succour, four.
Gas, alas, and Arkansas.
Sea, idea, Korea, area,
Psalm, Maria, but malaria.
Youth, south, southern, cleanse and clean.
Doctrine, turpentine, marine.

Compare alien with Italian,
Dandelion and battalion.
Sally with ally, yea, ye,
Eye, I, ay, aye, whey, and key.
Say aver, but ever, fever,
Neither, leisure, skein, deceiver.
Heron, granary, canary.
Crevice and device and aerie.

Face, but preface, not efface.
Phlegm, phlegmatic, ass, glass, bass.
Large, but target, gin, give, verging,
Ought, out, joust and scour, scourging.
Ear, but earn and wear and tear
Do not rhyme with here but ere.
Seven is right, but so is even,
Hyphen, roughen, nephew Stephen,
Monkey, donkey, Turk and jerk,
Ask, grasp, wasp, and cork and work.

Pronunciation—think of Psyche!
Is a paling stout and spikey?
Won't it make you lose your wits,
Writing groats and saying grits?
It's a dark abyss or tunnel:
Strewn with stones, stowed, solace, gunwale,
Islington and Isle of Wight,
Housewife, verdict and indict.

Finally, which rhymes with enough—
Though, through, plough, or dough, or cough?
Hiccough has the sound of cup.
My advice is to give up!!!

— Charivarious 1920s

---

A man who was deeply in debt
Said, 'No matter whatever I gebt,
My creditors claims
A share of the saim,
Which makes me discouraged, you bebt.

— *author unknown*

# SAYINGS FROM AROUND THE WORLD

## AFGHANISTAN

What you see in yourself is what you see in the world.
There are twenty-five uncaught sparrows for a penny.
Don't show me the palm tree, show me the dates.
Only stretch your foot to the length of your blanket.
No one says his own buttermilk is sour.

## ARGENTINA

No woman can make a wise man out of a fool, but every
woman can change a wise man into a fool.
If you have a tail of straw, then keep away from the fire.
A man who develops himself is born twice.
A dog that barks all the time gets little attention.

## BOSNIA & HERZEGOVINA

A brave man seldom is hurt in the back.
The eyes of all cheats are full of tears.
When an ant gets wings, it loses its head.
Two things rule the world — reward and punishment.
Why would you use poison if you can kill with honey.

## BRAZIL

A wise man learns at the fool's expense.
He who knows nothing, doubts nothing.
The trees with most leaves will not necessarily produce juicy
fruit.
Between the beginning and the end there is always a middle.
You can only take out of a bag what was already in it.

## BURMA

Beware of a man's shadow and a bee's sting.
The blind person never fears ghosts.
One sesame seed won't make oil.
A stupid act entails doing the work twice over.
A hero only appears once the tiger is dead.

## CHINA

A maker of idols is never an idolator.
A bird does not sing because it has an answer. It sings because it has a song.
A thorn defends the rose, harming only those who would steal the blossom.

## CZECH REPUBLIC

Wisdom is easy to carry but difficult to gather.
Better a lie which heals than a truth which wounds.
Nothing seems expensive on credit.
Do not protect yourself with a fence, but rather by your friends.

## DENMARK

A fool is like all other men as long as he remains silent.
Act honestly, and answer boldly.
Big words seldom accompany good deeds.
Faint hearts never win fair ladies.
Keep your nose out of another's mess.
Even a small star shines in the darkness.

## EGYPT

Learn politeness from the impolite.
When the angels present themselves, the devils abscond.
A beautiful thing is never perfect.
The barking of a dog does not disturb the man on a camel.

## FRANCE

A closed mouth catches no flies.
Desperate maladies require desperate remedies.
Hope is the dream of a soul awake.
He that spends more than he is worth spins a rope for his own neck.
A person who thinks evil of others should look into their own hearts.

## GERMANY

Too clever is stupid.
God gives the nuts, but he does not crack them.
Begin to weave and God will give the thread.
A lean agreement is better than a fat lawsuit.
Flatterers, like cats, lick and then scratch.

## GREECE

Great abilities produce great vices as well as virtues.
Men who have lost heart never yet won a trophy.
Men never moan over the opportunities lost to do good, only
the opportunities to be bad.
Milk the cow, but do not pull off the udder.
First secure an independent income, then practise virtue.

## HUNGARY

A prudent man does not make the goat his gardener.
The believer is happy; the doubter is wise.
When ambition ends, happiness begins.
Bargain like a gypsy, but pay like a gentleman.
A flatterer is a secret enemy.

## INDIA

Life is a bridge. Cross over it, but build no house on it.
A person consists of his faith. Whatever is his faith, even
so is he.
Don't bargain for fish which are still in the water.
Call on God, but row away from the rocks.
The cobra will bite you whether you call it cobra or Mr.
Cobra.

## IRAN

Listening to good advice is the way to wealth.
A blind man who sees is better than a sighted man who is
blind.
God provides, but He needs a nudge.
Every tear has a smile behind it.
Acquaintance without patience is like a candle with no light.

## IRELAND

He who gets a name for early rising can stay in bed until
midday.
Instinct is stronger than upbringing.
A trout in the pot is better than a salmon in the sea.
All sins cast long shadows.
The work praises the man.

## ITALY

To him that watches, everything is revealed.
To a quick question give a slow answer.
Better an egg today than a hen tomorrow.
Between saying and doing, many a pair of shoes is worn out.
The best armour is to keep out of range.

## JAPAN

You can't see the whole sky through a bamboo tube.
Time spent laughing is time spent with the gods.
Vision without action is a daydream; action without vision is
a nightmare.
Fall seven times, stand up eight.
Never rely on the glory of the morning or the smiles of your
mother-in-law.

## LEBANON

Hygiene is two thirds of health.
His brains hang at the top of his fez.
Do today what you want to postpone until tomorrow.
No matter how fast the poplar grows, it will never reach
heaven.
Lower your voice and strengthen your argument.

## MALAYSIA

He who has learned how to steal, must learn how to hang.
A fool is like the big drum that beats fast but does not realise
its hollowness.
To bend a bamboo, start when it is a shoot.
Do not measure another man's coat on your body.
The turtle lays thousands of eggs without anyone knowing,

but when the hen lays an egg, the whole country is
informed.

## MEXICO

As you see yourself, I once saw myself; as you see me
now, you will be seen.
Never ask God to give you anything; ask Him to put you
where things are.
He who strikes first, strikes twice.
It's not enough to know how to ride — you must also
know how to fall.

## NETHERLANDS

The seeds of the day are best planted in the first hour.
A handful of patience is worth more than a bushel of
brains.
He who attempts too much seldom succeeds.
Little pots soon run over.
God does not pay weekly, but He pays at the end.

## NEW ZEALAND

Turn your face to the sun and the shadows fall
behind you.
Boast during the day; be humble at night.
The block of wood should not dictate to the carver.
The more you ask how much longer it will take, the
longer the journey will seem.
Persist as resolutely as you persist in eating.

## NORWAY

It's no shame to look into the warm spring sun and regret
a lost limb.
It's too bad to want a thing and not be allowed it.
In every woman there is a Queen. Speak to the Queen
and the Queen will answer.
Rather a bit correctly than much incorrectly.
Luck is lent, not owned.

## PHILIPPINES

A clear conscience is far more valuable than money.

People who do not break things first will never learn to create anything.

If you make a habit of buying things you do not need, you will soon be selling things you do.

The rattan basket criticises the palm leaf basket, still both are full of holes.

## POLAND

The greatest love is a mother's, then a dog's, then a sweetheart's.

There are a thousand paths to every wrong.

God grant me a good sword and no use for it.

Even a clock that is not going is right twice a day.

Under capitalism man exploits man; under socialism the reverse is true.

## PORTUGAL

Beware of a man who does not talk and a dog that does not bark.

What was hard to bear is sweet to remember.

Hell is paved with good intentions, roofed in with lost opportunities.

Good management is better than good income.

Every peddler praises his own needles.

## RUSSIA

There is no shame in not knowing; the shame lies in not finding out.

Success and rest don't sleep together.

For him who does not believe in signs, there is no way to live in the world.

Acknowledgement is half of correction.

Pray to God, but keep rowing to the shore.

## SAUDI ARABIA

A book is a garden carried in the pocket.

Fear not the man who fears God.

A promise is a cloud; fulfilment is rain.

A little and a little, collected together, becomes a great deal; the heap in the barn consists of single grains, and drop and drop makes an inundation.

A friend is known when needed.

## SCOTTISH CULTURE

If you don't see the bottom, don't wade.

When the heart is full the tongue will speak.

Be slow in choosing a friend but slower in changing him.

Never let your feet run faster than your shoes.

Get what you can and keep what you have; that's the way to get rich.

## SOUTH AFRICA

If you are looking for a fly in your food,
it means that you are full.

He who has no intelligence is happy with it.

The fool who owns an ox is seldom recognised as a fool.

No hill without gravestones,
no valley without shadows.

You are not great just because you say you are.

## SPAIN

He who goes with wolves learns to howl.

How beautiful it is to do nothing, and then rest afterward.

The beginning of health is to know the disease.

More things grow in the garden than the gardener sows.

If you can't bite, don't show your teeth.

## SWEDEN

Fear less, hope more; eat less, chew more; whine less, breathe more; talk less, say more; hate less, love more; and all good things will be yours.

God gives every bird his worm, but he does not throw it into the nest.

Those who wish to sing always find a song.

## SWITZERLAND

When one shuts one eye, one does not hear everything.
Speech is silver; silence is golden.
One simple maxim is often worth more than two good friends.
When in doubt who will win, be neutral.
Better to sell with regret than to keep with regret.

## THAILAND

Bald people can always find a comb.
Life is so short we must move very slowly.
With one stump you can't make a good fire.
Wait until the tree has fallen before you jump over it.
At high tide the fish eat ants; at low tide the ants eat fish.

## TURKEY

Even though you know a thousand things, ask the man who knows one.
A person does not seek luck; luck seeks the person.
Coffee should be black as Hell, strong as death, and sweet as love.
Happiness is like crystal — when it shines the most, it soon cracks.

## UGANDA

He who hunts two rats, catches none
A roaring lion kills no game.
A strawberry blossom will not moisten dry bread.
Caution is not cowardice; even the ants march armed.

## VIETNAM

There is one fish in the pond, and ten anglers on the bank.
Venture all; see what fate brings.
The higher you climb, the heavier you fall.
Better to die than to live on with a bad reputation.

## WELSH CULTURE

Three things give us hardy strength: sleeping on hairy mattresses, breathing cold air, and eating dry food.
Conscience is the nest where all good is hatched.

Your hand is never the worse for doing it's own work.
Without perseverance talent is a barren bed.

## YIDDISH CULTURE

If God wants people to suffer, he sends them too much understanding.
If you want your dreams to come true, don't oversleep.
Before you start up a ladder, count the rungs.
If a link is broken, the entire chain breaks.
He who can't endure the bad will not live to see the good.

## ZEN CULTURE

If you understand, things are just as they are; if you do not understand, things are just as they are.
Sitting quietly, doing nothing, spring comes and the grass grows by itself.
Do not seek the truth, only cease to cherish your opinions.

# DID YOU KNOW?

Those markings found on dice are called *pips*.

Words misinterpreted in a song are called *mondegreen*.

When the planets of our solar system line up it's called a *syzygy*.

The side of a hammer is called the *truck*.

Mountains form by a process called *orogeny*.

Flammable and inflammable mean the same thing.

A heavy winter's fog containing ice crystals is called a *pogonip*.

# LANGUAGE PROVERBS

A child when it begins to speak
learns what it is that it knows — *Norwegian proverb*

Every definition is dangerous — *Latin proverb*

Signposts only show the road, they don't go along it
— *Swiss German proverb*

Word to deed is if from leaf to root — *Serbian proverb*

Fair words butter no parsnips.

Good words make us laugh, good deeds make us silent
— *French proverb*

Words shake but examples attract — *Serbian proverb*

A child learns quicker to talk than to be silent
— *Norwegian proverb*

Our language is one great salad — *Romanian proverb*

A hen that crows and a woman who knows Latin never come
to a good end — *Spanish proverb*

# WHY IS IT THAT
# LONG IS SHORTER THAN SHORT?

And short is longer than long?
Why is long not longer than short
And short not shorter than long?

Why is not shorter shorter than short,
As longer is longer than long?
And why is longer shorter than shorter
And shorter not shorter than long?

If shorter was short and short was shorter,
Then shorter'd be shorter than short.
But if long were longer and longer were long
Then longer'd be shorter than long.

I hereby suggest that shorter be long
And longer be shorter instead.
Then long would be longer
Thus longer than short
And short could be just as it was.

But if longer is shorter, is shorter longer,
And shorter not long as I said?
And if long is now longer and shorter now long,
Is short still as short as it was?

Can longer be shorter, whilst shorter is long,
Or is shorter now longer not long?
And if long is now longer and shorter is long,
Is long not shorter as well?
—*author unknown*

# RHETORICAL MYSTERIES

*These linguistic mysteries are posed in question form as an end in themselves ... their purpose is to puzzle, to mystify and add to the mystique of our language.*

Whose cruel idea was it for the word lisp to have an s in it?

How come abbreviation is such a long word?

Why is there only one word for thesaurus?

Why are they called buildings, when they're already finished? Shouldn't they be called builts?

Why are there 5 syllables in the word monosylabic?

Why is it, when a door is open it's ajar, but when a jar is open, it's not adoor?

If con is the opposite of pro, then what is the opposite of progress?

Why do we wait until a pig is dead to cure it?

I went to a bookstore and asked the saleswoman, "Where's the self-help section?" She said if she told me, it would defeat the purpose.

Can you be a closet claustrophobic?

Why is bra singular and panties plural?

\* \* \* \* \* \*

# RULE BREAKERS

The rule being I before E except after C

Ei's that break the rule

| | | |
|---|---|---|
| albeit | cuneiform | eiderdown |
| alzheimer | decaffeinate | eisteddfod |
| apartheid | deionised | either |
| caffeine | deionises | fahrenheit |
| caffeinic | deionising | feisty |
| codeine | edelweiss | foreign |
| counterfeit | eider | forfeit |

194

forfeiting
forfeits
forfeiture
Fraulein
geiger
geisha
heifer
height
heir
herein
hereinafter
hereinto
heterogeneity
homogeneity
inveigle
inveigling
kaleidoscope
kinaestheic
leisure
leitmotifs
madeiras
meioses

monseigneur
nuclei
obeisance
onomatopoeia
plebeian
pleistocene
poltergeist
pre-industrial
protein
reveille
ribonucleic
seige
seigneur
seismic
seizable
seize
seizure
sheik
sheikh
sheila
simultaneity
sobeit

spontaneity
stein
sovereign
speiled
surfeit
surveillance
their
theirs
therein
thereinafter
unveil
veil
veiled
weiner
weir
weird
weirdo
wherein
whereinsoever
zeitgeist

## Ie's that break the rule

ancient
bioscience
boccie
coefficient
cogencies
concierge
conscience
conscientious
curacies
deficiency
deficient
efficient

facie
financier
gaiety
geoscientist
geoscientists
glacier
hacienda
inefficient
insufficiencies
insufficient
intersocietal

neuroscience
omniscient
prescience
proficient
science
society
species
subspecies
sufficient
testacies
unscientific

# SAME SOUND, DIFFERENT SPELLING

*When you stop to consider all the ways we have of arriving at the same sound, it's really quite wondrous.*

*Here are some examples of the variety of ways the same sound can be achieved with different spelling.*

## Long E+R sound
**ear:** dear, ear, fear, gear, hear, near, rear, sear, tear, year, clear.

**eer:** beer, deer, jeer, leer, queer, peer, veer, steer, career.

**ere:** here, mere, interfere.

**ier:** bier, tier.

## Long A+T sound
**ate:** ate, bate, date, fate, gate, hate, late, mate, pate, rate, sate, rotate.

**ait:** bait, gait, wait.

**eat:** great.

**eight:** eight, freight, weight.

## Long A+N sound
**ane:** bane, cane, lane, mane, pane, plane, sane, vane, wane.

**ain:** chain, drain, gain, main, pain, rain, vain, slain, explain, detain, remain, contain, refrain, maintain.

**eign:** deign, feign, reign.

**ein:** rein, vein.

## Long E+N sound
**een:** between, careen, seen, teen, keen, preen, spleen, queen.

**ean:** bean, dean, lean, mean, wean, clean.

**ene:** scene, gene, neoprene, kerosene, carotene.

**ine:** gasoline, dexodrine, magazine.

## Long A + L sound

**ale:** ale, bale, dale, hale, gale, kale, male, pale, sale, tale, whale, vale.

**ail:** ail, bail, fail, flail, hail, jail, mail, nail, pail, rail, sail, snail, tail, wail, retail.

**eil:** veil.

## Long A+R sound

**air:** fair, hair, lair, stair, chair, pair, affair, repair, unfair

**are:** care, dare, bare, fare, hare, mare, pare, ware, beware, rare, scare, tare

**ear:** bear, wear, tear, pear

## Long A+M sound

**aim:** aim, maim.

**ame:** came, blame, dame, lame, game, fame, name, same, tame.

## Long U+T sound

**ute:** brute, flute.

**oot:** boot, coot, hoot, loot, moot, root, shoot, scoot, toot.

## Long I+N sound

**ign:** sign, align.

**ine:** brine, dine, fine, line, mine, nine, pine, sine, tine, wine, refine, confine.

## Long U+N sound

**une:** dune, rune, tune.

**oon:** boon, croon, goon, loon, moon, noon, soon, spoon.

## Long O+L sound

**ole:** dole, hole, pole, sole, vole.

**owl:** bowl.

**oll:** knoll, poll, roll, toll, troll.

**oul:** soul.

**oal:** foal, goal.

# AS CLEAR AS CRYSTAL

*For those who'd like to know what is like what
... a list of similes in common usage.*

As agile as a monkey
As bald as a baby's backside
As bald as a coot
As big as a bus
As big as an elephant
As black as a sweep
As black as coal
As black as one is painted
As black as pitch
As blind as a bat
As blind as a mole
As bold as brass
As brave as a lion
As bright as a button
As bright as a new pin
As bright as day
As busy as a beaver
As busy as a bee
As calm as a millpond
As clear as a bell
As clean as a hound's tooth
As clean as a whistle
As clear as crystal
As cold as ice
As common as dirt
As cool as a cucumber
As crazy as a loon
As cunning as a fox
As cute as a button
As cute as a cup cake
As dead as a doornail

As dead as the dodo
As deaf as a post
As delicate as a flower
As dense as a brick
As different as chalk from
  cheese
As drunk as a lord
As dry as a bone
As dry as dust
As dull as dishwater
As easy as A.B.C.
As easy as pie
As fat as a pig
As fit as a fiddle
As flat as a pancake
As free as a bird
As fresh as a daisy
As gentle as a lamb
As good as gold
As happy as a clown
As happy as a lark
As happy as Larry
As happy as a rat with a gold
  tooth
As hard as nails
As high as a kite
As hoarse as a crow
As hot as hell
As hungry as a bear
As hungry as a wolf
As innocent as a lamb

As keen as mustard
As large as life
As light as a feather
As light as air
As lowly as a worm
As mad as a hatter
As mad as a hornet
As mad as the march hare
As merry as a cricket
As modest as a maiden
As much use as a yard of
pump water
As naked as a baby
As neat as a pin
As nutty as a fruitcake
As obstinate as a mule
As old as the hills
As pale as death
As patient as Job
As plain as day
As pleased as Punch
As poor as a church mouse
As poor as dirt
As pretty as a picture
As proud as a peacock
As pure as snow
As pure as the driven snow
As quick as a wink
As quick as lightning
As quick as silver
As right as rain
As safe as houses
As scarce as hen's teeth
As sensitive as a flower
As sharp as a needle
As sharp as a razor

As sick as a dog
As sick as a parrot
As silent as the dead
As silly as a goose
As slippery as an eel
As slow as molasses
As slow as a snail
As slow as a tortoise
As slow as a wet weekend
As smooth as silk
As snug as a bug in a rug
As sober as a judge
As soft as a baby's bottom
As solid as a rock
As solid as the ground we
stand on
As sound as a bell
As sour as vinegar
As steady as a rock
As sticky as jam
As stiff as a board
As still as death
As straight as an arrow
As strong as an ox
As stubborn as a mule
As sturdy as an oak
As sure as death and taxes
As sweet as honey
As tall as a giraffe
As tight as a drum
As thick as a brick
As thin as a rake
As thin as a toothpick
As timid as a rabbit
As tough as leather
As tough as nails

As tough as old boots
As tricky as a box of monkeys
As welcome as a skunk at a
   lawn party
As white as snow

As wise as Solomon
As white as a ghost
As white as a sheet
As wise as an owl

# YE OLDE SPELL CHECKER

Eye halve a spelling checker
It came with my pea sea
It plainly marks four my revue
Miss steaks eye kin knot sea.
Eye strike a key and type a word
And weight four it two say
Weather eye am wrong oar write
It shows me strait a weigh.
As soon as a mist ache is maid
It nose bee fore two long
And eye can put the error rite
It's rare lea ever wrong.
Eye Have run this poem threw it
I am shore your pleased two no
Its letter perfect awl the weigh
My checker tolled me sew.

*—author unknown*

# LOST IN TRUNCATION

*This Short Message Service (SMS) is the new language of a whole generation who are finding shorthand code to send messages, sometimes many dozens a day, to their friends via the mobile phone and Net Messenger services.*

2U2 *To You,Too*
ASL? *Age sex location?*
AAMOF *As A Matter Of Fact*
AFAIC *As Far As I'm Concerned*
AFAICT *As Far As I Can Tell*
AFAIK *As Far As I Know*
AFK *Away from keyboard*
ASAP *As Soon As Possible*
BAK *Back at the keyboard*
BBL *Be back later*
BITMT *But In The Meantime*
BOT *Back On Topic*
BFN *Bye For Now*
BG *Big Grin*
BRB *Be Right Back*
BS *bullshit*
BTA *But Then Again*
BTW *By The Way*
CU/CYA *See You*
CUL(8R) *See You Later*
C4N *Ciao For Now*
CRS *Can't Remember Stuff*
CWOT *Complete Waste Of Time*
DITYID *Did I Tell You I'm Distressed?*
DIY *Do It Yourself*
DIKY *Do I Know You?*
EOD *End Of Discussion*
EZ *Easy*

EOT *End Of Threat*
F2F *Face To Face*
FAQ *Frequently Asked Questions*
FBOW *For Better Or Worse*
FOAF *Friend Of A Friend*
FOCL *Falling Off Chair Laughing*
FWIW *For What It is Worth*
FYA *For Your Amusement*
FYI *For Your Information*
GA *Go Ahead*
GAL *Get A Life*
GBTW *Get Back To Work*
GFC *Going For Coffee*
GFETE *Grinning From Ear To Ear*
GMTA *Great Minds Think Alike*
GR&D *Grinning, Running & Ducking*
GTG *Got To Go*
GTGTTBR *Got To Go To The Bathroom*
GTRM *Going To Read Mail*
HAND *Have A Nice Day*
HHOK *Ha Ha Only Kidding*
HTH *Hope This Helps*
IAC *In Any Case*
IAE *In Any Event*
IC *I See*
ICQ *I seek You*

IDGI *I Don't Get It*
IMCO *In My Considered Opinion*
IMHO *In My Humble Opinion*
IMNSHO *In My Not So Humble Opinion*
IMO *In My Opinion*
IMVHO *In My Very Humble Opinion*
IOTTMCO *Intuitively Obvious To The Most Casual Observer*
IOW *In Other Words*
IRL *In Real Life*
ISP *Internet Service Provider*
IYKWIM *If You Know What I Mean*
JIC *Just In Case*
J/K *Just Kidding*
J4F *Just for Fun*
KISS *Keep It Short and Simple/Keep It Simple Stupid*
L8R *Later*
LD *Later Dude*
LTNS *Long Time No See*
LOL *Laughing Out Loud*
MorF *Male or Female*
MTCW *My Two Cents Worth*
NRN *No Reply Necessary*
NIFOC *Naked In Front of Computer*
OBTW *O By The Way*
ONNA *Oh No, Not Again!*
OTOH *On The Other Hand*
OTTOMH *Off The Top Of My Head*

OIC *Oh I See*
OTF *On The Floor*
OLL *Online Love*
PCMCIA *People Can't Memorise Computer Industry Acronyms*
PLS *Please*
PU *That Stinks!*
PITA *Pain In The Ass*
Q *Question*
REHI *Hello Again (re-Hi!)*
ROFL *Rolling On Floor Laughing*
ROTF *Rolling On The Floor*
ROTFLMAO *Rolling On The Floor Laughing My Ass Off*
RSN *Real Soon Now*
RTDox *Read The Documentation/Directions*
RUOK *Are You OK?*
SNAFU *Situation Normal; All Fouled Up*
SO *Significant Other*
SOL *Smiling Out Loud*
TAFN *That's All For Now*
TGIF *Thank God It's Friday*
THX *Thanks*
TY *Thank You*
Txs *Thanks*
TANSTAAFL *There Ain't No Such Thing As A Free Lunch*
TEOTWAWKI *The End Of The World As We Know It*
TIA *Thanks In Advance*
TLK2UL8R *Talk To You Later*
TMK *To My Knowledge*
TOS *Terms Of Service*
TPTB *The Powers That Be*

TSWC *Tell Someone Who Cares*
TTBOMK *To The Best Of My Knowledge*
TTFN *Ta-Ta For Now*
TTYL(8R) *Talk To You Later*
TWIMC *To Whom It May Concern*
URL *Web Page Address*
VBG *Very Big Grin*
W/B *Welcome Back*
WRT *With Regard To*
WWW *World Wide Web*
W8 *Wait*

WTG *Way To Go!*
WU? *What's Up?*
WYSIWYG *What You See Is What You Get*
Y2K *Year 2000*
YW *You're Welcome*
YGIAGAM *Your Guess Is As Good As Mine*
YGWYPF *You Get What You Pay For*
YMMV *Your Mileage May Vary*
ZZZ *Sleeping*

# BEFUDDLED?

*Bravery / Bravado / Bravura*
Bravery denotes a brave action or person.
Bravado means ostentatious boldness or courage.
Bravura means a showy way of playing in music or some other field of endeavour.

*Climatic / Climactic / Climacteric*
Climatic means 'relating to climate'
Climactic means 'building to a climax'
Climacteric denotes 'the period in life when fertility and sexual interest are in decline.

*Ostensible / Ostensive / Ostentatious*
Ostensible means professed or apparent.
Ostensive, rarer cousin, means directly demonstrated.
Ostentatious means showy and pretentious.

# PUNCTUATION CHALLENGE

*Try putting the quote marks and full stops into this sentence given as a punctuation challenge in an exam. The solution is directly below.*

Marjorie had had had had while Bartholomew had had had had had had the teacher's approval.

And here's the solution in case you were struggling:

*Marjorie had had 'had had', while Bartholomew had had 'had'   'Had had' had had the teacher's approval.'*

## COMPUTER WOES!

If the label on the cable on the table at your house,
Says the network is connected to the button on your mouse,
But your packets want to tunnel on another protocol,
That's repeatedly rejected by the printer down the hall,
And your screen is all distorted by the side effects of gauss,
So your icons in the window are as wavy as a souse,
Then you may as well reboot and go out with a bang,
'Cause as sure as I'm a poet, the sucker's gonna hang!

If your cursor finds a menu item followed by a dash,
And the double-clicking icon puts your window in the trash,
And your data is corrupted 'cause the index doesn't hash,
then your situation's hopeless, and your system's gonna crash!

— *author unknown*

# MORE LANGUAGE PROVERBS

Where argument fails, try abuse.

A lie will go around the world
while truth is pulling its boots on.

A promise is a bridge of words, unsafe to walk across
— *German proverb*

Sit crooked but speak straight — *Turkish proverb*

The pen of the tongue should be dipped in the ink of the heart
— *Italian proverb*

Silence is wisdom, when speaking is folly.

Beware of a man who doesn't talk and a dog who doesn't bark.

Think much, speak little and write less.

A kind word warms for three winters — *Chinese proverb*

A honey tongue, a heart of gall — *Portuguese proverb*

One must let people talk, since fish can't — *Polish proverb*

The eyes have one language everywhere.

# TONGUE TWISTERS

*A tongue twister is a collection of words deliberately designed
to be hard to articulate...They send your tongue tripping,
tugging and twirling tentatively.*

A bitter biting bittern
Bit a better brother bittern,
And the bitter better bittern
Bit the bitter biter back.

\*   \*   \*

A gazillion gigantic grapes gushed
gradually giving gophers gooey guts.

\*   \*   \*

Betty Botter bought some butter but she said, 'the butter's
bitter. If I put it in my batter it will make my batter bitter.'
So she bought some better butter, better than the bitter
butter, and she put it in her batter and her batter was not
bitter. So 'twas good that Betty Botter bought some better
butter.

\*   \*   \*

Brisk brave brigadiers brandished broad bright blades,
blunderbusses, and bludgeons balancing them badly.

\*   \*   \*

Can you imagine an imaginary menagerie manager imagining
managing an imaginary menagerie?

\*   \*   \*

Federal Express is now called FedEx.
When I retire I'll be a FedEx ex.
But if I'm an officer when I retire, I'll be an ex Fedex Exec.
Then after a divorce, my ex-wife will be an ex FedEx exec's ex.
If I rejoin FedEx in time, I'd be an ex ex FedEx exec.
When we remarry, my wife will be an ex ex FedEx exec's ex.

\*   \*   \*

How much ground would a groundhog hog, if a groundhog
could hog ground? A groundhog would hog all the ground he
could hog, if a groundhog could hog ground.

*   *   *

I thought a thought.
But the thought I thought wasn't
the thought I thought I thought.
If the thought I thought I thought
had been the thought I thought,
I wouldn't have thought so much.

*   *   *

If a Hottentot taught a Hottentot tot
To talk ere the tot could totter,
Ought the Hottenton tot
Be taught to say aught, or naught,
Or what ought to be taught her?

I'm a mother pheasant plucker.
I pluck mother pheasants.
I'm the pleasantest mother pheasant plucker,
That ever plucked a mother pheasant.
I'm not the fig plucker,
Nor the fig plucker's son,
but I'll pluck your figs
till the fig plucker comes.

*   *   *

Larry Hurley, a burly squirrel hurler, hurled a furry squirrel
through a curly grill.

*   *   *

Mary Mac's mother's making Mary Mac marry me.
My mother's making me marry Mary Mac.
Will I always be so merry when Mary's taking care of me?
Will I always be so merry when I marry Mary Mac?

*   *   *

Moses supposes his toeses are roses,
but Moses supposes erroneously.
For Moses, he knowses his toeses aren't roses,
as Moses supposes his toeses to be.

\*   \*   \*

Peter Piper picked a peck of pickled peppers.
If Peter Piper picked a peck of pickled peppers,
Where's the peck of pickled peppers Peter Piper picked?

\*   \*   \*

Ruby Rugby's brother bought and brought her
back some rubber baby-buggy bumpers.

\*   \*   \*

She is a thistle-sifter. She has a sieve of unsifted thistles and
a sieve of sifted thistles and the sieve of unsifted thistles she
sifts into the sieve of sifted thistles because she is a thistle-sifter.

\*   \*   \*

These sheep shouldn't sleep in a shack;
sheep should sleep in a shed.

\*   \*   \*

Sister Suzie sewing shirts for soldiers
Such skill as sewing shirts
Our shy young Sister Suzie shows
Some soldiers send epistles
Say they'd rather sleep in thistles
Than the saucy, soft short shirts for soldiers Sister Suzie sews.

\*   \*   \*

Something in a thirty-acre thermal thicket of thorns and
thistles thumped and thundered threatening the three-D
thoughts of Matthew the thug — although, theatrically, it
was only the thirteen-thousand thistles and thorns through
the underneath of his thigh that the thirty-year-old thug
thought of that morning.

\*   \*   \*

The ruddy widow really wants ripe watermelon and red roses
when winter arrives.

\* \* \*

The bottle of perfume that Willy sent
Was highly displeasing to Millicent.
Her thanks were so cold
That they quarreled, I'm told
O'er that silly scent Willy sent Millicent.

\* \* \*

The seething seas ceaseth
And twiceth the seething seas sufficeth us.

\* \* \*

There once was a man who had a sister, his name was Mr.
Fister. Mr. Fister's sister sold sea shells by the sea shore. Mr.
Fister didn't sell sea shells, he sold silk sheets. Mr. Fister told
his sister that he sold six silk sheets to six sheiks. The sister
of Mr. Fister said I sold six shells to six sheiks too!

\* \* \*

Three grey geese in the green grass grazing.
Grey were the geese and green was the grass.

\* \* \*

Three tree turtles took turns talking tongue twisters.
If three tree turtles took turns talking tongue twisters,
Where's the twisters the three tree turtles talked?

\* \* \*

To sit in solemn silence in a dull dark dock
In a pestilential prison with a life long lock
Awaiting the sensation of a short sharp shock
From a cheap and chippy chopper on a big black block.

\* \* \*

When the copy of your floppy's getting sloppy on the disk,
And the microcode instructions cause unnecessary risk,
Then you have to flash your memory and you'll want to ram
your rom.

Whether the weather be fine
or whether the weather be not.
Whether the weather be cold
or whether the weather be hot.
We'll weather the weather
whether we like it or not.

\*    \*    \*

Yellow butter, purple jelly, red jam, black bread.
Spread it thick, say it quick!

Yellow butter, purple jelly, red jam, black bread.

Spread it thicker, say it quicker!
Yellow butter, purple jelly, red jam, black bread.
Don't eat with your mouth full!

\*    \*    \*    \*

You've no need to light a night-light
On a light night like tonight,
For a night-light's light's a slight light,
And tonight's a night that's light.
When a night's light, like tonight's light,
It is really not quite right
To light night-lights with their slight lights
On a light night like tonight.

## SHORT BUT DEADLY

We reweave rips
Free flea spray
The sun shines on shop signs
She said she should sit
Three free throws.

# TOM PUN

*Tom Swifties are a certain punny wordplay — Tom, or someone of another name, makes a statement followed by an adverb or some descriptive word tacked on which is a play on the previous words it's a pun. Are you ready?*

## A

"I'm wearing my wedding ring," said Tom with abandon.

"I'm concerned about the number of people not attending," said Tom absent-mindedly.

"Who would want to steal modern art?" asked Tom abstractedly.

"Now I can chop down that tree," said Tom with a heavy accent.

"Let's all play an A, a C sharp, and an E," cried Tom's band with one accord.

"I gave the donkey some vinegar," said Tom acidly.

## B

"Give me a haircut," Tom said barbarously.

"I've been listening to the Brandenberg Concertos," Tom barked.

"I'm losing my hair!" Tom bawled.

"I have to keep this fire alight," Tom bellowed.

"Are you all governors?" Tom asked, bored.

"I still haven't struck oil," said Tom boringly.

## C

"There's nothing to stop me putting things in tins," said Tom cannily.

"It's a bloody lion," said Tom categorically.

"I love the novels of D.H. Lawrence," said the lady chattily.

"I was completely exonerated," said Tom clearly.

"The prisoner escaped down a rope," said Tom condescendingly.

"I organised that big party for the prisoners," Tom confessed.

## D

"I've had these Beardsley prints for ten years," said Tom decadently.

"I can no longer see anything," said Tom delightedly.

When butchers meet, Tom always delivers a speech — but he hams it up.

"We've just brought gold and frankincense," the Magi demurred.

"Don't let me drown in Egypt!" pleaded Tom, deep in denial.

## E

"Let's get married," said Tom engagingly.

"What a charming doorway!" said Tom, entranced.

"I wouldn't marry you if you were the only woman on earth," said Tom evenly.

"My former wife is cute," said Tom expertly.

## F

"This is the Netherlands," Tom stated flatly.

"This steamroller really works," said Tom flatteringly.

"I'm falling into a void," said Tom flawlessly.

"I've joined the navy," Tom said fleetingly.

"Ignore the first three turnings," said Tom forthrightly.

"I didn't see that French 'No Smoking' sign," fumed Tom defensively.

## G

"This house is in good taste!" said Hansel and Gretel gingerly.

"This food tastes of plutonium," said Tom glowingly.

"For what we are about to receive, may the Lord make us truly thankful," said Tom gracefully.

"My wife is dead", said Prince Rainier gracelessly.

"Would anyone like some Parmesan?" asked Tom gratingly.

"It's just gold leaf," said Tom guiltily.

## H

"I only have diamonds, clubs and spades," said Tom heartlessly.

"I've been to San Francisco" said Tom heartlessly.

"It's my maid's night off," said Tom helplessly.

"I was the first to climb Mount Everest," said Tom hilariously.

"Nay!" said Tom hoarsely.

"I have to keep these eggs warm," Tom chirped honestly.

"The doctors had to remove a bone from my arm," said Tom humorlessly.

## I

"She's burning aromatic substances," said Tom, incensed.

"I don't want to drown in Paris!" pleaded Tom insanely.

"I'm not leaving the chapel until I finish this painting," said Michelangelo insistently.

"I like camping," said Tom intently.

"This is my assessment," said Tom irately.

## K

"My parents are called Billy and Nanny," Tom kidded.

"I've run out of wool," said Tom, knitting his brow.

## L

"I refuse to make an agenda," Tom said listlessly.

"It's where we store the hay," Tom said loftily.

"I always pray to St. Ignatius," said Tom loyally.

"I chop down trees for a living," said Tom lumberingly.

## M

"I'm just going to put these handcuffs on you,"
said Tom manically.

"It's only average," said Tom meanly.

"It's hard work arresting that girl!" said Tom, labouring
under a misapprehension.

"Do you call this a musical?" asked Les miserably.

"The girl's been kidnapped," said Tom mistakenly.

"I'm tired of smiling," moaned Lisa.

## N

"I haven't developed my photographs yet," said Tom negatively.

"That just doesn't add up," said Tom, nonplussed.

"What's the value of a dollar bill?" asked Tom noteworthily.

## O

"That horse looks like a good bet at 17 to 1," said Tom oddly.

"My wrists are bleeding stumps!" said Tom offhandedly.

"I prefer trout to salmon," Tom said officiously.

"It's half a score," Tom said often.

"My bicycle wheel is damaged," said Tom outspokenly.

## P

"I've joined the Airborne Medical Corps," said Tom
paradoxically.

"Ici nous voyons le tour Eiffel!" Tom parried.

"I'm waiting to see the doctor," said Tom patiently.

"I wish I had something to write with," Tom said pensively.

"I need to clear my throat," said Tom phlegmatically.

"The cat seems happy now it's been fed," said Tom purposefully.

# Q

"This is where I keep my arrows," said Tom, quivering.

# R

"There it is again!" Tom recited.

"It's time for the second funeral," Tom rehearsed.

"I've gone back to my wife," was Tom's rejoinder.

"I've passed the exam this time," Tom remarked.

"I've an urgent appointment," said Tom in Russian.

# S

"I'll use my stopwatch to see how fast it moves," said Tom, seconding the motion.

"The optician probably doesn't have my glasses ready yet," Tom speculated.

"Yes, I have read Gulliver's Travels," said Tom swiftly.

# T

"Parsley, sage, rosemary," said Tom timelessly.

"I'm going to fix the roof," Tom translated.

"I was adopted," said Tom transparently.

# U

"I'm not sure about Heisenberg," said Tom uncertainly.

"I won't stand for painting," said Tom uneasily.

"I want to date other women," said Tom unsteadily.

# V

"So that's the way the wind blows," said Tom vainly.

"This is a picture of my new house," said Tom, visibly moved.

# W

"I'm always exhausted by Friday," said Tom weakly.

"I'm not a real man," Tom whimpered.

"I wish I'd said that, Oscar," said Tom wildly.

"I've read all Shakespeare's works," said Tom wilfully.

"Some you lose," said Tom winsomely.

## Z

"I can't eat any more lemon peel," said Tom zestfully.

"Your fly is undone," was Tom's zippy rejoinder.

---

## PUNNY ANSWERS

What is the difference between a train and a tree?
*One leaves its shed — the other sheds its leaves.*

Why is it hard to keep a secret in the winter?
*Because your teeth chatter.*

What colour is the wind?
*Blew.*

What is the difference between the death of a barber
and the death of a sculptor?
*One curls up and dyes — the other makes faces and
busts.*

# WAYS TO SAY— *I LOVE YOU*

*Now tell them how you feel, but if you want to be a little mysterious or devious, say it in another language!*

| | |
|---|---|
| **Arabic** | Ana Behibak (to a male) |
| **Arabic** | Ana Behibek (to a female) |
| **Bavarian** | I mog di narrisch gern |
| **Bulgarian** | Obicham te |
| **Burmese** | chit pa de |
| **Cambodian** | Bon sro lanh oon |
| **Canadian French** | Sh'teme |
| **Cantonese** | Ngo oi ney |
| **Chinese** | (see the entries for mandarin or cantonese!) |
| **Corsican** | Ti tengu cara (to female) |
| **Corsican** | Ti tengu caru (to male) |
| **Croatian** | LJUBim te |
| **Czech** | miluji te |
| **Danish** | "Jeg elsker dig" (pronounced 'yai el-ske die') |
| **Dutch** | Ik hou van jou |
| **English** | I love you |
| **Filipino** | Mahal ka ta |
| **Flemish** | Ik zie oe geerne |
| **French** | Je t'aime |
| **Gaelic** | Ta gra agam ort |
| **German** | Ich liebe Dich |
| **Greek** | S'ayapo |
| **Hawaiian** | Aloha I'a Au Oe |
| **Hebrew** | Ani ohev otach (male to female) |
| | Ani ohev otcha (male to male) |
| | Ani ohevet otach (female to female) |
| | Ani ohevet otcha (female to male) |
| **Hindi** | Mai tumase pyar karata hun (male to female) |
| **Hindi** | Mai tumase pyar karati hun (female to male) |
| **Hungarian** | Szeretlek |
| **Icelandic** | Eg elska thig |

| | |
|---|---|
| **Indonesian** | Saya cinta padamu |
| **Iranian** | Mahn doostaht doh-rahm |
| **Irish** | Taim i' ngra leat |
| **Italian** | ti amo (if it's a relationship/lover/spouse) |
| **Japanese** | Kimi o ai shiteru |
| **Korean** | Tangsinul sarang ha yo |
| **Latin** | Te amo |
| **Lebanese** | Bahibak |
| **Lithuanian** | Tave Myliu |
| **Mandarin** | Wo ai ni |
| **Norwegian** | Eg elskar deg (Nynorsk) |
| **Pakistani** | Mujhe Tumse Muhabbat Hai |
| **Persian** | Tora dost daram |
| **Polish** | Kocham Cie |
| **Portuguese** | Amo-te |
| **Punjabi** | Mai taunu pyar karda |
| **Romanian** | Te iu besc |
| **Russian** | Ya tebya liubliu |
| **Serbian** | Ljubim te |
| **Slovak** | lubim ta |
| **Spanish** | Te amo |
| **Srilankan** | Mama Oyata Arderyi |
| **Swahili** | Naku penda |
| **Swedish** | Jag a'lskar dig |
| **Swiss-German** | Ch'ha di ga"rn |
| **Syrian/Lebanese** | Bhebbek (to a female) |
| | Bhebbek (to a male) |
| **Tahitian** | Ua Here Vau Ia Oe |
| **Thai** | Khao Raak Thoe |
| **Tunisian** | Ha eh bak |
| **Turkish** | Seni seviyorum |
| **Ukrainian** | Ja tebe koKHAju |
| **Vietnamese** | Em yêu anh (woman to man) |
| | Anh yêu em (man to woman) |
| **Welsh** | 'Rwy'n dy garu di. |
| **Yiddish** | Ich libe dich |
| **Yugoslavian** | Ya te volim |
| **Zulu** | Mena Tanda Wena |

# LINGUISTIC LINGO

*The following is a glossary of the terms from this book, explaining the meaning of the word plays or terminology, with examples provided.*

**ACRONYM**: Abbreviation using the initial letters of a series of words.
Example: ASAP is *as soon as possible.*

**ALLITERATION**: is the repetition of initial consonant sounds.
Example: the alliteration of "m" in
*"The moan of doves in immemorial elms,*
*And murmuring of innumerable bees."*
　　— Alfred Lord Tennyson

**ANAGRAM**: ways of moving the letters around from one word to form one word or more that have meaning.
Examples:  T. S. Eliot  becomes *toilets.*
Margaret Thatcher becomes *that charmer.*

**ANTONYM:** the opposite of a term.
Example: *Cleave* is a rare word because two of its synonyms are antonyms — *adhere* and *split apart.*

**APTONYM**: where people's names have a close link to their occupations.
Examples: *David Bird* ornithologist; *Jett Black* hairdresser

**BUZZWORD**: usually a jargon term designed to sound important but often pure chaff.
Example: *corporate culture, paradigm shift.*

**CLICHÉ**: a trite stereotyped expression, idea or practice. It originated as a French printing term, a metal plate used for printing the image rather than text and could be used time and time again, as it was.
Examples: *it's not rocket science; at the end of the day.*

**COLLECTIVE NOUNS**: are words for groups of people, animals, objects.
Examples: *herd of elephants*; *swarm of bees.*

**EPITAPH**: inscription on a tombstone which is traditionally in verse form but can have exceptions.
Example: On John Yeast, *Here lies Johnny Yeast, Pardon me for not rising.*

**EPONYM**: a person's name which has become a word for something, or the name of a law.
Example: *bloomers* after Amelia Bloomer, US women's rights activist.

**EUPHEMISM**: is a way of making the meaning of words less embarrassing or unpleasant.
Examples: *passed away, went to meet his maker* and *negative patient outcome* are all euphemisms for death.

**IDIOM**: is an expression whose meaning is not predictable from the usual meaning of the constituent words.
Examples: *to kick the bucket* meaning dying; *tickled pink* meaning to be delighted.

**MNEMONICS (pronounced with the first 'm' silent)**:
Memory aids which are in words form, all sorts.
Example: for remembering the order of planets from the Sun out, remembering Pluto's demotion to a dwarf planet.
*My Very Efficient Manager Just Sends Us Nuts!*
Mercury, Venus, Earth, Mars, Jupiter, Saturn, Uranus, Neptune

**NEOLOGISM**: Newly coined or invented word or phrase.
Examples: *sheeple* for people who act like sheep; *hippycrite* an erstwhile hippy who's gone all conservative in middle age.

**ONOMATOPOEIA**: Words which imitate the sound of the words they mean.
Examples: *Buzz, clang, murmur.*

**OXYMORON** (plural, oxymora): Contradiction in terms and usually used deliberately
Examples: *Friendly fire, creation science.*

**PALINDROME**: A sequence of units, usually words or phrases that can be read front-to-back and back-to-front.
Examples: *Glenelg*, coastal suburb in Adelaide, Australia; *Able was I ere I saw Elba*, Napoleon supposedly.

**PANGRAM**: Sentence containing every letter in the alphabet
Example: *The quick brown fox jumped over the lazy dog.*

**PLEONASM**: The antonym or opposite of an oxymoron containing one or more words that are simply reinforcing the first word's meaning.
Examples: *PIN number* and *free gift.*

**PORTMANTEAU (plural portmanteaux)**: Forming a new word from two others and blending their meaning into one.
Example: *Motel* from motor + hotel.

**PROVERB**: An apt saying which has often become credible through its widespread use. It's usually practical wisdom in a nutshell. Example: *Least said, soonest mended.*

**PUN**: A humorous play on the similar sound of words.
Example: *Do it for the pun of it!*

**SIMILE**: In this book, similes take on a structure. The quality of hardness or clarity or softness is likened to something, using the formula, "as .... as ..........".
Example: *As empty as a pub on Christmas Day.*

**TONGUE TWISTER**: A collection of words designed to be difficult to articulate well.
Example: *She sells seashells by the seashore.*

# SPEAKING OF WORDS

*Here are a choice collection of quotes on words and language, some chosen for their wryness of wit, others for their deep profound insights.*

There was nothing wrong with her that a vasectomy of the vocal cords wouldn't fix. — *Lisa Ather*

Man does not live on bread alone, his other necessity is communication. — *Charles F Hockett*

Brevity is the sister of talent.
— *Anton Chekhov*

If I write four words, I strike out three of them.
— *A M Moliére*

Let thy speech be better than silence, or be silent.
— *Dionysus the Elder*

Diplomacy is the art of saying "Nice doggie!" until you can find a rock.
— *Wynn Catlin*

Apology is only egotism wrong side out.
— *Oliver Wendell Holmes ,Sr*

Flattery is  false coin that is only current thanks to our vanity. — *Duc de la Rochefoucald*

Flattery is alright, if you don't inhale.
— *Adlai Stevenson*

It is all too rare today to hear the clear, clean ring of an original insult. — *Jim Richard Carrigan*

Disagreement may be the shortest cut between two minds.
— *Kahlil Gibran*

Propaganda is that branch of the art of lying which consists
in nearly deceiving your friends without quite deceiving your
enemies. — *Francis Cornford*

An exaggeration is a truth that has lost its temper.
— *Kahlil Gibran*

White lies are but the gentleman ushers to black ones.
— *Frederick Marryat*

Reading makes a full man, meditation a profound man,
discourse a clear man.
— *Benjamin Franklin*

Language, the most valuable single possession of the human
race. — *Charles F Hockett*

Never speak more clearly than you think.
— *Howard Henry Baker*

Thought is no more identical with language
than feeling is identical to the nervous system.
— *Samuel Butler*

Words are organised thoughts, as living forms are organised
actions. — *Samuel Butler*

I see grammar as the first part in the art of thinking.
— *Ettienne de Condillac*

First learn the meaning of what you say,
then speak.
— *Epictetus*

Thought flies and words go on foot, therein lies all the drama
of a writer. — *Julian Green*

A moment's thinking is an hour in words.
— *Thomas Hood*

This is one of the disadvantages of wine, it makes a man
mistake words for thoughts. — *Samuel Johnson*

Questions show the minds range, and answers its subtlety.
— *Joseph Joubert*

Ideas are enclosed and almost bound in words like precious
stones in a ring. — *Giacomo Leopardi*

Labels are devices for saving talkative people from thinking.
— *John Morley*

Language is not outside the mind ... but is the outside of the
mind — *Thomas Hood*

Most thinkers write badly because they communicate not only
their thoughts, but also the thinking of them.
— *Frederick Nietzsche*

When people cease to complain, they cease to think.
— *Napoleon*

When things have taken hold of the mind, the words come
crowding forth. — *Lucius Aeneas Seneca*

My words fly up, my thoughts remain below,
words without thoughts never to heaven go.
— *William Shakespeare*

Speech was given to man to disguise his thoughts.
— *Charles Maurice de Tallyrand*


Think like a wise man,
but express yourself like the common people.
— *W B Yeats*


Language does not leave fossils,
at least until it has become written.
— *Richard Brautigan*


To man alone of all existing beings was speech given, because
for him alone was it necessary. —*Dante*


Voice developed in the trees, gesture on the ground.
— *J R Firth*


What a good thing Adam had.
When he said a good thing
he knew nobody had said it before.
— *Mark Twain*


Error is never so difficult to be destroyed when it has its root
in language. — *Jeremy Bentham*


A definition is the enclosing of a wilderness of idea within a
wall of words. — *Samuel Butler*


Take care of the sense and the sounds will take care of
themselves. — *Lewis Carroll*

The meaning of the word is not in the word, they are in us.
— *S I Hayakawa*

Meanings receive their dignity from words, instead of giving
it to them. — *Blaise Pascal*

Everything's been said, no doubt. If words hadn't changed
meaning, and meaning words. — *Jean Paulhan*

Meanings are not things, not even very queer things.
— *Gilbert Ryle*

I confused things with their names: that is belief.
— *Jean Paul Sartre*

Words may be deeds. — *Aesop*

A man of words but not of deeds
Is like a garden full of weeds.
— *Mother Goose nursery rhymes*

Language moves down time in a current of its own making.
— *Edward Sapir*

The individual, in his use of language,
has constantly to improvise.
— *Otto Jesperson*

I have crossed an ocean
I have lost my tongue
From the root of an old one
A new one has sprung.
— *Grace Nichols*

Reading is to the mind what exercise is to the body.
— *Richard Steele*

That woman speaks eighteen languages
and can't say "No" in any of them.
— *Dorothy Parker*


Translation is at best an echo. — *George Borrow*


Translations, like wives,
are seldom faithful if they are in the least attractive.
— *Roy Campbell*


What's in a name? That which we call a rose

By any other word would smell as sweet.

— *William Shakespeare*, Romeo and Juliet


Language is a process of free creation; its laws and principles
are fixed, but the manner in which the principles of
generation are used is free and infinitely varied.

Even the interpretation and use of words involves a process of
free creation.

— *Noam Chomsky*


People demand freedom of speech as a compensation for the
freedom of thought which they seldom use.

— *Soren Kierkegaard*


Women speak because they wish to speak, whereas a
man speaks only when driven to speech by something
outside himself — like, for instance, he can't
find any clean socks.
— *Jean Kerr*

Her voice was ever soft
Gentle and low
An excellent thing in woman.
— *King Lear of Cordelia, William Shakespeare*

It isn't what I do, but how I do it.
It isn't what I say, but how I say it—
and how I look when I do and say it.
— *Mae West*

To listen closely and reply well
is the highest perfection we are able to attain
in the art of conversation.
— *Duc de la Rochefoucald*

Listening is one of the lesser-known skills
that mistresses offer.
— *Betty Jane Wylie*

What is reading but silent conversation?
— *Walter Savage Landor*

Chapters reveal the mind. — *Lawrence Sterne*

Reading is seeing by proxy. — *Herbert Spencer*

Writers, like teeth, are divided into incisors and grinders.
— *Walter Bagehot*

Kindness: a language the deaf
can hear and the blind can see.
— *Unknown*

The pen is the tongue of the hand
— a silent utterer for  the eye.
— *Henry Ward Beecher*

Drawing on my fine command of language,
I said nothing.
— *Robert Benchley*

No iron can stab the heart with such force as a full stop
put just in the right place.
— *Isaac Babel*

Our language has wisely sensed
the two sides of being alone.
It has created the word,
loneliness to express the pain of being alone.
And it has created the word,
solitude to express the glory of being alone.
— *Paul Tillich*

It's a damn poor mind that can only think of one way
to spell a word.
— *Andrew Jackson*

Man is a creature who lives not upon bread alone, but
primarily by catchwords.
— *Robert Louis Stevenson*

The limits of my language
mean the limits of my world.

— *Ludwig Wittgenstein*

When I read some of the rules for speaking and writing the
English language correctly, I think any fool can make a rule,
and every fool will mind it.

— *Henry David Thoreau*

# INDEX